September 12 '90
Happy F

Joyce & Mark

Our Proud Past

by Gail J. McCormick

A Compiled History of the Families
that Settled at the End of the Oregon Trail

VOLUME ONE

Copyright 1993 by
Gail J. McCormick Publishing Company
P. O. Box 1200
Mulino, Oregon 97042-1200

Our Proud Past, Volume I
First Revised Edition
First Printing
A Printing of 5,000 Copies
Printed in U.S.A.
All Rights Reserved

ISBN 0-9635889-1-5

Our Proud Past

Volume One

by Gail J. McCormick

First Revised Edition

First Printing

Printed to Commemorate the Oregon Trail Pioneers

This book is dedicated to those
who have been the constant
loving factor in my adult life —

my three children:

Joy, Lisa and Bill

Table of Contents

Author's Preface

Two years ago, that sly fox, "Destiny," tapped my shoulder ever so lightly. I say sly because, since then, others have told me "I was planning to do what you are doing." And that was, recording the history of my area in, what I call, "a proper form." But, destiny was slyer with me than others. He had every intention of succeeding this time.

He offered me the first temptation to write this history when neighbor, Harvey Gambell, phoned and said "Would you like to write a story about the beginning of the Mulino Water Department?" During our interview, I discovered an exceptionally interesting person, and then Harvey presented me with the "coupe de resistance" and that was the old pictures he showed me. Next, came a phone call from a relative of Ed Engle, saying I should try to see him, that he knew a lot of history, was ill and his time with us was limited. So, I phoned Ed, and we "got together". The viewing of his grandparent's picture, the Engle family, took me a step further back in time and the need to seek historical knowledge slowly developed into an almost insatiable desire.

I dropped most of my social relationships with people under the age of 70 — they had become boring — and started spending more time with the older generation. Although single, no suitor lasted long against this force. Those who made it to my living room sofa were barraged with my latest find of historical pictures and tales I had heard. They soon were seen retreating back down the trail from whence they had just come, barely noticed by me, for I had found something I enjoyed more than the company of the opposite sex. My true blue friends were offered chances to paste up stories with me to the wee hours of morning. No need for a clock on this venture. True blue's were soon offering to meet me in town for a drink — Mulino was "too far out to come."

Like an actor who starts living his part, I began to live in that time. Yes, I was there when that first whip cracked to move the wagon train out to the unknown Oregon wilderness in 1843. I cried when that child was buried in the wagon wheel tracks. I was with that lonely, determined pioneer, William Hatchette Vaughan, when he hoisted his wagon over the Oregon City bluffs. I felt the anguish of the pioneer woman, Lizzie Wright, as she took care of her family, struck down by smallpox. I tasted the "soda water" at Wilhoit Springs and saw, for the first time, that puff of steam from Hell over yonder, that turned out to be Bagby Hot Springs. I hunkered down in the tall grasses and waited patiently with John Bagby for that bear to get up on the high log and look for danger. I rode on the sunny, grassy knoll with Horace Dibble and decided there was no prettier place on earth to build the Dibble House. I was on that first train that puffed into Molalla in 1913 and I have sat in on that first wild "shoot 'em up" Molalla Buckeroo Rodeo.

Ah, yes, the pessimist would try to spoil my fun and say I am only imagining this . . . although I have become a bit more eccentric than most, there will always be historians like myself. For as long as time goes on, there will be those who have more of a desire to look back than look ahead. There will be those who eagerly poke into that corner closet, trying to find an old picture album that will show what went on before them. There will be those "history buffs" who've just got to "feel" how it was then. I have yet to determine how we became this way, but it may have been an interest cultured by another person.

My desire, with this book, is to help instill that interest in others and assist each reader in feeling what it was like to live in a time when life moved slowly and seemed so much more rewarding.

And so, I present what I have lived and loved these past two years . . .

Our Proud Past

"Campground", William Henry Jackson drawing.

CHAPTER I

The First

Wagon Train Out

Crossing the South Platte. "A mile wide and a foot deep."
William Henry Jackson painting.
Courtesy of NPS/Scotts Bluff National Monument

Bibliography:
Applegate, Jesse, "Day With the Cow Column", <u>Oregon Historical Quarterly</u>, December, 1900
Nesmith, James W., "Diary of Emigration of 1843", <u>Oregon Historical Quarterly</u>, December, 1906

PART ONE:

"A Day with the Cow Column in 1843"

by Jesse Applegate

Jesse Applegate was a participant in the first wagon train out. The following is reprinted in its entirety from the Oregon Historical Quarterly, December, 1900.

"The migration of a large body of men, women and children across the continent to Oregon was, in the year 1843, strictly an experiment; not only in respect to the members, but to the outfit of the migrating party. Before that date, two or three missionaries had performed the journey on horseback, driving a few cows with them. Three or four wagons drawn by oxen had reached Fort Hall, on Snake River, but it was the honest opinion of the most of those who had traveled the route down Snake River, that no large number of cattle could be subsisted on its scanty pasturage, or wagons taken over a country so rugged and mountainous.

"The emigrants were also assured that the Sioux would be much opposed to the passage of so large a body through their country, and would probably resist it on account of the emigrants' destroying and frightening away the buffaloes, which were then dimishing in numbers.

"The migrating body numbered over one thousand souls, with about one hundred and twenty wagons, drawn by six-ox teams, averaging about six yokes to the team, and several thousand loose horses and cattle.

"The emigrants first organized and attempted to travel in one body, but it was soon found that no progress could be made with a body so cumbrous, and as yet so averse to all discipline. And at the crossing of the 'Big Blue' it divided into two columns, which traveled in supporting distance of each other as far as Independence Rock on the Sweetwater.

"From this point, all danger from Indians being over, the emigrants separated into small parties better suited to the narrow mountain paths and small pastures in their front.

"Before the division on the Blue River there was some just cause for discontent in respect to loose cattle. Some of the emigrants had only their teams, while others had large herds in addition, which must share the pasture and be guarded and driven by the whole body. This discontent had its effect in the division on the Blue. Those not encumbered with or having but few loose cattle attached themselves to the light column; those having more than four or five cows had of necessity to join the heavy or cow column. Hence the cow column, being much larger than the other and much encumbered with its large herds, had to use greater exertion and observe a more rigid discipline to keep pace with the more agile consort. It is with the cow column that I propose to journey with the reader for a single day.

"It is four o'clock a.m.; the sentinels on duty have discharged their rifles - the signal that the hours of sleep are over - and every wagon and tent is pouring forth its night tenants, and slow-kindling smokes begin largely to rise and float away in the morning air. Sixty men start from the corral, spreading as they make through the vast herd of cattle and horses that make a semicircle around the encampment, the most distant perhaps two miles away.

"The herders pass to the extreme verge and carefully examine for trails beyond, to see that none of the animals have strayed or been stolen during the night. This morning no trails led beyond the outside animals in sight, and by 5 o'clock the herders begin to contract the great, moving circle, and the well-trained animals move slowly towards camp, clipping here and there a thistle or a tempting bunch of grass on the way. In about an hour five thousand animals are close up to the encampment, and the teamsters are busy selecting their teams and driving them inside the corral to be yoked. The corral is a circle one hundred yards deep, formed with wagons connected strongly with each other; the wagon in the rear being connected with the wagon in front by its tongue and ox chains. It is a strong barrier that the most vicious ox cannot break, and in case of an attack of the Sioux would be no contemptible entrenchment.

"From 6 to 7 o'clock is a busy time; breakfast is to be eaten, the tents struck, the wagons loaded and the teams yoked and brought up in readiness to be attached to their respective wagons. All know when, at 7 o'clock, the signal to march sounds, that those not ready to take their proper places in the line of march must fall into the dusty rear for the day.

"There are sixty wagons. They have been divided into fifteen divisions or platoons of four wagons each, and each platoon is entitled to lead in its turn. The leading platoon today will be the rear one tomorrow, and will bring up the rear unless some teamster, through indolence or negligence, has lost his place in the line, and is condemned to that uncomfortable post. It is within ten minutes of seven; the corral but now a strong barricade is everywhere broken, the teams being attached to the wagons. The women and children have taken their places in them. The pilot (a borderer who has passed his life on the verge of civilization and has been chosen to the post of leader from his knowledge of the savage and his experience in travel through roadless wastes), stands ready, in the midst of his pioneers and aids, to mount and lead the way. Ten or fifteen young men, not today on duty, form another cluster. They are ready to start on a buffalo hunt, are well mounted and well armed, as they need be, for the unfriendly Sioux have driven the buffalo out of the Platte, and the hunters must ride fifteen or twenty miles to reach them. The cow drivers are hastening, as they get ready, to the rear of their charge, to collect and prepare them for the day's march.

"It is on the stroke of seven; the rush to and fro, the cracking of whips, the loud command to oxen, and what seemed to be the inextricable confusion of the last ten minutes has ceased. Fortunately every one has been found and every teamster is at his post. The clear notes of a trumpet sound in the front; the pilot and his guards mount their horses; the leading division of the wagons move out of the encampment, and take up the line of march; the rest fall into their places with the precision of clock work, until the spot so lately full of life sinks back into that solitude that seems to reign over the broad plain and rushing river as the caravan draws its lazy length towards the distant El Dorado. It is with the hunters we shall briskly canter towards the bold but smooth and grassy bluffs that bound the broad valley, for we are not yet in sight on the grander but less beautiful scenery (of Chimney Rock, Court House and other bluffs, so nearly resembling giant castles and palaces), made by the passage of the Platte through the highlands near Laramie. We have been traveling briskly for more than an hour. We have reached the top of the bluff, and now have turned to view the wonderful panorama spread before us. To those who have not been on the Platte, my powers of description are wholly inadequate to convey an idea of the vast extent and grandeur of the picture, and the rare beauty and distinctness of the detail. No haze or fog obscures objects in the pure and transparent atmosphere of this lofty region. To those accustomed only to the murky air of the seaboard, no correct judgement of distance can be formed by sight, and objects which they think they can reach in a two hours' walk may be a day's travel away; and though the evening air is a better conductor of sound, on the high plain during the day the report of the loudest rifle sounds little louder than the bursting of a cap; and while the report can be heard but a few hundred yards, the smoke of the discharge may be seen for miles. So extended is the view from the bluff on which the hunters stand, that the broad river glowing under the morning sun like a sheet of silver, and the broader emerald valley that borders it, stretch away in the distance until they narrow at almost two points in the horizon, and when first seen, the vast pile of the Wind River Mountains though hundreds of miles away, looks clear and distinct as a white cottage on the plain.

"We are a full six miles away from the line of march; though everything is dwarfed by distance, it is seen distinctly. The caravan has been about two hours in motion and is now as widely extended as a prudent regard for safety will permit. First, near the bank of the shining river is a company of horsemen; they seem to have found an obstruction, for the main body has halted while three or four ride rapidly along the bank of the creek or slough. They are hunting a favorable crossing for the wagons; while we look they have succeeded; it has apparently required no work to make it passable, for all but one of the party have passed on, and he has raised a flag, no doubt a signal to the wagons to steer their course to where he stands. The leading teamster sees him, though he is yet two miles off, and steers his course directly towards him, all the wagons following in his track. They (the wagons) form a line three-quarters of a mile in length; some of the teamsters ride upon the front of their wagons, some march beside their teams; scattered along the line companies of women are taking exercise on foot; they gather bouquets of rare and beautiful flowers that line the way; near them stalks a stately greyhound, or an Irish wolf dog, apparently proud of keeping watch and ward over his master's wife and children. Next comes a band of horses; two or three men or boys follow them, the docile and sagacious animals scarce needing this attention, for they have learned to follow in the rear of the wagons, and know that at noon they will be allowed to

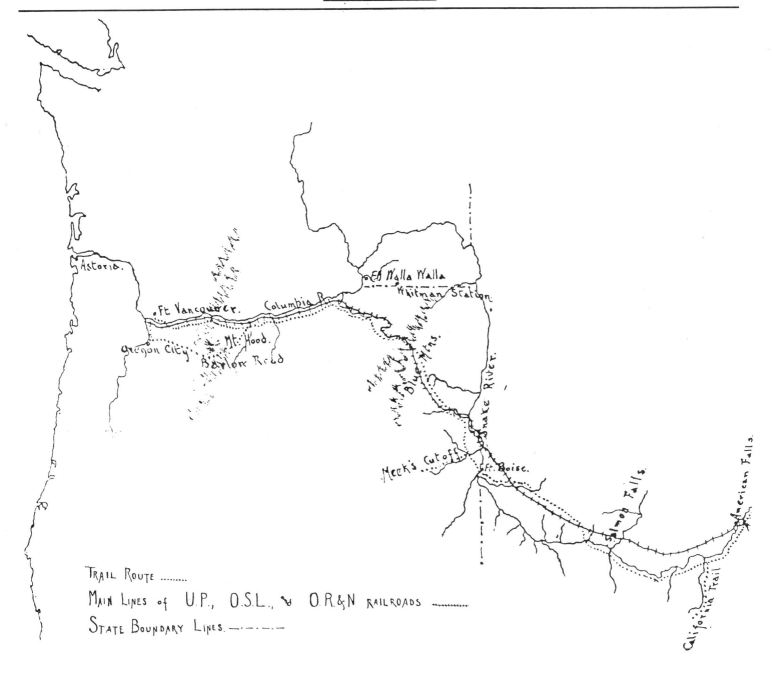

The Oregon Trail:
First part of simply drawn map from Oregon Historical Quarterly, December, 1906

graze and rest. Their knowledge of time seems as accurate as of the place they are to occupy in the line and even a full-blown thistle will scarce tempt them to straggle or halt until the dinner hour has arrived. Not so with the large herd of horned beasts that bring up the rear; lazy, selfish and unsocial, it has been a task to get them in motion, the strong always ready to domineer over the weak, halt in the front and forbid the weak to pass them. They seem to move only in the fear of the driver's whip; though in the morning, full to repletion, they have not been driven an hour before their hunger and thirst seem to indicate a fast of days' duration. Through all the long day their greed is never satisfied, nor their thirst quenched, nor is there a moment of relaxation of the tedious and vexatious labors of their drivers, although to all others the march furnishes some season of relaxation

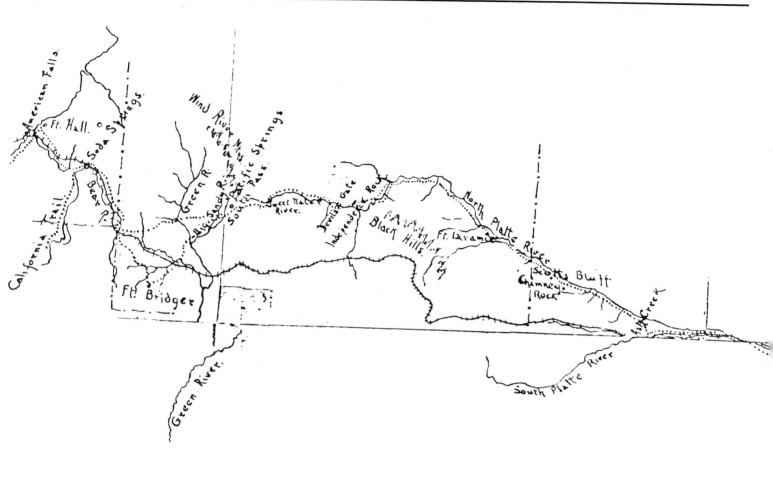

TRAIL ROUTE ....

MAIN LINES of U.P., O.S.L., & O.R.&N RAILROADS ....

STATE BOUNDARY LINES. —..—..—

The Oregon Trail:
Second part of simply drawn map from Oregon Historical Quarterly, December, 1906

or enjoyment. For the cow-drivers there is none.

"But from the standpoint of the hunters, the vexations are not apparent; the crack of whips and loud objurgation are lost in the distance. Nothing of the moving panorama, smooth and orderly as it appears, has more attractions for the eye than that vast square column in which all colors are mingled, moving here slowly and there briskly, as impelled by horsemen riding furiously in front and rear.

"But the picture in its grandeur, its wonderful mingling of colors and distinctness of detail, is forgotten in contemplation of the singular people who give it life and animation. No other race of men with the means at their command would undertake so great a journey, none save these could successfully perform it, with no previous preparation, relying only on the fertility of their own invention to devise the means to overcome each danger

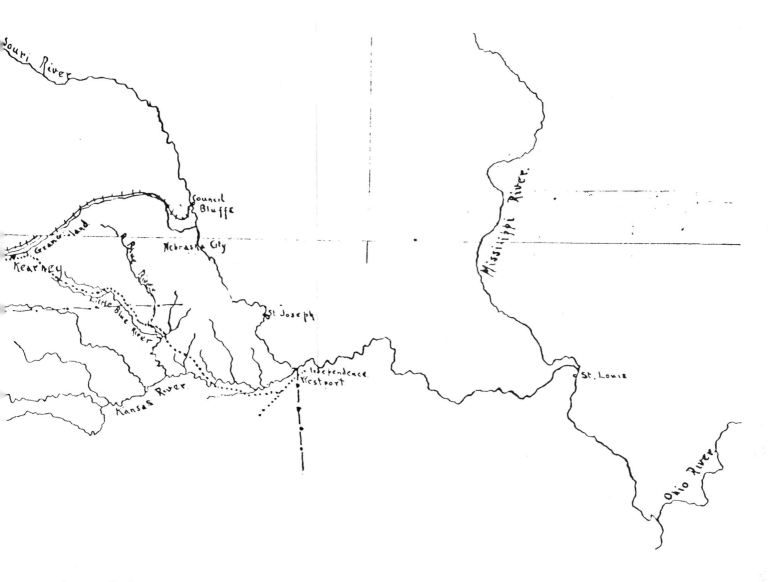

The Oregon Trail:
Third part of simply drawn map from Oregon Historical Quarterly, December, 1906

and difficulty as it arose. They have undertaken to perform with slow-moving oxen a journey of two thousand miles. The way lies over trackless wastes, wide and deep rivers, ragged and lofty mountains, and is beset with hostile savages. Yet, whether it were a deep river with no tree upon its banks, a rugged defile where even a loose horse could not pass, a hill too steep for him to climb, or a threatened attack of an enemy, they are always found ready and equal to the occasion, and always conquerors. May we not call them men of destiny? They are people changed in no essential particulars from their ancestors, who have followed closely on the footsteps of the receding savage, from the Atlantic seaboard to the great Valley of the Mississippi.

"But while we have been gazing at the picture in the valley, the hunters have been examining the high plain in the other direction. Some dark moving objects have been discovered in the distance, and all are closely watching them to discover what they are, for in the atmosphere of the plains a flock of crows marching miles away, or a band of buffaloes or Indians at ten times the distance look alike, and many ludicrous mistakes occur. But these are buffaloes, for two have stuck their heads together and are, alternately, pushing each other back. The hunters mount and away in pursuit, and I, a poor cow-driver, must hurry back to my daily toil, and take a scolding from my fellow herders for so long playing truant.

"The pilot, by measuring the ground and timing the speed of the wagons and the walk of his horses, has determined the rate of each, so as to enable him to select the nooning place, as nearly as the requisite grass and water can be had at the end of five hours' travel of the wagons. Today, the ground being favorable, little time has been lost in preparing the road, so that he and his pioneers are at the nooning place an hour in advance of the wagons, which time is spent in preparing convenient watering places for the animals, and digging little wells near the bank of the Platte, as the teams are not unyoked, but simply turned loose from the wagons, a corral is not four abreast, the leading wagon of each platoon on the left, the platoons being formed with that in view. This brings friends together at noon as well as at night.

"Today an extra session of the council is being held, to settle a dispute that does not admit of delay, between a proprietor and a young man who has undertaken to do a man's service on the journey for bed and board. Many such engagements exist, and much interest is taken in the manner in which this high court, from which there is no appeal, will define the rights of each party in such engagements. The council was a high court in the most exalted sense. It was a senate composed of the ablest and most respected fathers of the emigration. It exercised both legislative and judicial powers, and its laws and decisions proved it equal and worthy of the high trust reposed in it. Its sessions were usually held on days when the caravan was not moving. It first took the state of the little commonwealth into consideration; revised or repealed rules defective or obsolete, and enacted such others as the exigencies seemed to require. The common weal being cared for, it next resolved itself into a court to hear and settle private disputes and grievances. The offender and the aggrieved appeared before it; witnesses were examined, and the parties were heard by themselves and sometimes by counsel. The judges being thus made fully acquainted with the case, and being in no way influenced or cramped by technicalities, decided all cases according to their merits. There was but little use for

lawyers before this court, for no plea was entertained which was calculated to hinder or defeat the ends of justice. Many of these judges have since won honors in higher spheres. They have aided to establish on the broad basis of right and universal liberty two pillars of our great Republic in the Occident. Some of the young men who appeared before them as advocates have themselves sat upon the highest judicial tribunals, commanded armies, been governors of states and taken high position in the senate of the nation.

"It is now one o'clock; the bugle has sounded and the caravan has resumed its westward journey. It is in the same order, but the evening is far less animated than the morning march; a drowsiness has fallen apparently on man and beast; teamsters drop asleep on their perches and even when walking by their teams, and the words of command are now addressed to the slowly creeping oxen in the soft tenor of women or the piping treble of children, while the snores of the teamsters make a droning accompaniment. But a little incident breaks the monotony of the march. An emigrant's wife, whose state of health has caused Doctor Whitman to travel near the wagon for the day, is now taken with violent illness. The Doctor has had the wagon driven out of the line, a tent pitched and a fire kindled. Many conjectures are hazarded in regard to this mysterious proceeding, and as to why this lone wagon is to be left behind. And we too must leave it, hasten to the front and note the proceedings, for the sun is now getting low in the west and at length the painstaking pilot is standing ready to conduct the train in the circle which he has previously measured and marked out, which is to form the invariable fortification for the night. The leading wagons follow him so nearly around the circle that but a wagon length separates them. Each wagon follows in its track, the rear closing on the front, until its tongue and ox-chains will perfectly reach from one to the other, and so accurate the measure and perfect the practice, that the hindmost wagon of the train always precisely closes the gateway, as each wagon is brought into position. It is dropped from its team (the teams being inside the circle), the team unyoked and the yokes and chains are used to connect the wagon strongly with that in its front. Within ten minutes from the time the leading wagon halted, the barricade is formed, the teams unyoked and driven out to pasture. Every one is busy preparing fires of buffalo chips to cook the evening meal, pitching tents and otherwise preparing for the night. There are anxious watchers for the absent wagon, for there are many matrons who may be afflicted like its inmate before the journey is over; and they fear the strange and startling practice of this Oregon doctor will be dangerous. But as the sun goes down the absent wagon rolls into camp, the bright, speaking face and cheery look of the doctor, who rides in advance, declare without words that all is well, and both mother and child are comfortable. I would fain now and here pay a passing tribute to that noble and devoted man, Doctor Whitman. I will obtrude no other name upon the reader, nor would I his were he of our party or even living, but his stay with us was transient, though the good he did was permanent, and he has long since died at his post.

"From the time he joined us on the Platte until he left us at Fort Hall, his great experience and indomitable energy were of priceless value to the migrating column. His constant advice, which we knew was based upon a knowledge of the road before us, was, 'Travel, travel, travel; nothing else will take you to the end of your journey; nothing is wise that does not help you along; nothing is good for you that causes a moment's delay.' His great authority as a physician and complete success in the case above referred to, saved us many prolonged and perhaps ruinous delays from similar causes, and it is no disparagement to others to say that to no other individual are the emigrants of 1843 so much indebted for the successful conclusion of their journey as to Dr. Marcus Whitman.

"All able to bear arms in the party have been formed into three companies, and each of these into four watches; every third night it is the duty of one of these companies to keep watch and ward over the camp, and it is so arranged that each watch takes its turn of guard duty through the different watches of the night. Those forming the first watch tonight will be second on duty, then third and fourth, which brings them through all the watches of the night. They begin at 8 o'clock p.m., and end at 4 o'clock a.m.

"It is not yet 8 o'clock when the first watch is to be set; the evening meal is just over, and the corral now free from the intrusion of cattle or horses, groups of children are scattered over it. The larger are taking a game of romps; "the wee toddling things" are being taught that great achievement that distinguishes man from the lower animals. Before a tent near the river a violin makes lively music, and some youths and maidens have improvised a dance upon the green; in another quarter a flute gives its mellow and melancholy notes to the still night air, which, as they float away over the quiet river, seem a lament for the past rather than a hope for the future. It has been a prosperous day; more than twenty miles have been accomplished of the great journey. The encampment is

a good one; one of the causes that threatened much future delay has just been removed by the skill and energy of that 'good angel' of the emigrants, Doctor Whitman, and it has lifted a load from the hearts of the elders. Many of these are assembled around the good doctor at the tent of the pilot (which is his home for the time being), and are giving grave attention to his wise and energetic counsel. The care-worn pilot sits aloof, quietly smoking his pipe, for he knows the brave doctor is 'strengthening his hands'.

"But time passes; the watch is set for the night; the council of old men has been broken up, and each has returned to his own quarter; the flute has whispered its last lament to the deepening night; the violin is silent, and the dancers have dispersed; enamored youth have whispered a tender 'good night' in the ear of blushing maidens, or stolen a kiss from the lips of some future bride - for Cupid here, as elsewhere, has been busy bringing together congenial hearts and among these simple people he alone is consulted in forming the marriage tie. Even the doctor and the pilot have finished their confidential interview and have separated for the night. All is hushed and repose from the fatigues of the day, save the vigilant guard and the wakeful leader, who still has cares upon his mind that forbid sleep. He hears the 10 o'clock relief taking post and the 'all well' report of the returned guard; the night deepens, yet he seeks not the needed repose. At length a sentinel hurries to him with the welcome report that a party is approaching - as yet too far away for its character to be determined, and he instantly hurries out in the direction in which it was seen. This he does both from inclination and duty, for in times past the camp had been unnecessarily alarmed by timid or inexperienced sentinels, causing much confusion and fright amongst women and children, and it had the authority to call out the military strength of the column, or of so much of it as was in his judgment necessary to prevent a stampede or repel an enemy. Tonight he is at no loss to determine that the approaching party are our missing hunters, and that they have met with success, and he only waits until by some further signal he can know that no ill has happened to them. This is not long wanting. He does not even await their arrival, but the last care of the day being removed, and the last duty performed, he too seeks the rest that will enable him to go through the same routine tomorrow.

"But here I leave him, for my task is also done, and unlike his, it is to be repeated no more."

*　*　*

"Approaching Chimney Rock", William Henry Jackson painting.
Courtesy of NPS/Scotts Bluff National Monument

PART TWO:

"Diary of the Emigration of 1843"

by James W. Nesmith

The following is reprinted from the Oregon Historical Society Quarterly, December, 1906. At the time of the writing of this diary, James W. Nesmith was 23 years of age.

"Thursday, May 18, 1843. - The Oregon company met at the grove West of Fitzhugh's Mill on May 18, 1843. The meeting was organized by calling Mr. Layson to the chair, and Mr. Burnett secretary. It was moved and seconded that there be a committee of nine appointed to draft rules and regulations to govern the company. Resolved, that a committee of seven be appointed for the purpose of inspecting the outfits of the different individuals comprising the company.

"Saturday, May 20. - After several days preparatory arrangements, we agreed to rendezvous at the spring near Fitzhugh's Grove.

"Sunday, May 21. - Cooper's wagons, with some others, start out from the encampment in the morning. I go to Fitzhugh's Mill with Squire Burnett and others to see the committee and Captain Gantt, in order to ascertain what arrangements had been made to secure the captain's services as pilot. This day was fine and clear. Took a farewell look at the State of Missouri. We overtook the wagons at a grove of timber, south of the Santa Fe Trail, where we encamped for the night.

"Monday, May 22. - Trailed to Elm Grove, distance about ten miles. Encamped at the grove, consisting of one old elm stump, which the Sante Fe traders had chipped and trimmed for the purpose of procuring wood to cook with.

"Tuesday, May 23. - Traveled about ten miles on the trail, then turned to the right and encamped about one mile from the trail at some timber near a small creek, distance about twelve miles.

"Wednesday, May 24. - Pursued our way towards Kansas River. Traveled about twelve miles. Let our wagons down the bank of the Rockariski (Wakarusa) River and encamped on the west side. On this evening, Captain Gantt, the pilot, came into camp. Weather fine.

"Thursday, May 25. - Traveled about fifteen miles to a creek. Some of the wagons encamped on each side.

"Friday, May 26. - Arrived at Kansas. Crossed the river on a platform made of two canoes. Encamped on the northwest side, at the landing. I swam the river several times with ease, and once assisted a young man named Wm. Vaughn to shore. Another man assisted me. His name was G. W. Stewart. Came near drowning myself in consequence of Vaughn's struggling with me in the water. Camped on Soldier Creek, two miles from Kansas Landing until we first organized and elected Peter Burnett captain and self orderly sergeant. Moved about five miles and encamped on the banks of the Kansas River, in a square. My duty required me to take the names of men for duty. They numbered 254. The number of wagons was 111.

"Friday, June 9. - We moved from the wet encampment about two miles, and encamped about noon at a small grove of timber south of the trail. The weather cleared up about noon. We divided our company into four divisions and elected a captain and orderly sergeant for each. Sergeant Ford on guard.

"Saturday, June 10. - Left the encampment about 8:00 o'clock. I went on with the advance guard. About 11;00 o'clock came up to where a dead Indian lay on the prairie, with his head cut off and his body much mutilated. Supposed to have been done by the late Kansas war party against the Pawnees. We picked up some arrows on the ground. Traveled about ten miles and encamped at a grove on the North side of the trail. All prairie to-day. The weather fine and the roads wet and soft. Sergeant Gilmore on guard.

"Sunday, June 11. - Left camp about 8:00 o'clock. Weather fine. I traveled in advance with the pilot and advance guard. Time passed agreeably. Company moved on well, considering the soft condition of the ground. Passed the California wagons about 1:00 o'clock. Saw but little timber on the trail, but some in sight on the south side of Blue River, which we have been traveling up for four days. leaving the main fork from two to four miles on our left hand. Camped at night on the west side of Horse Creek, after a day's travel of fourteen miles. Rained in the evening. Had a great deal of difficulty crossing the creek, some of the company remaining on the opposite side all night.

"Monday, June 12. - Left the encampment about 10:00 o'clock, this detainment occurred in consequence of some of the wagons being detained in crossing. I went on with the pioneers or advance guard. About 12:00 o'clock I discovered a buffalo on a ridge about two miles north of the trail. Captain Gantt, myself, and four others started in pursuit of him. He, in the meantime, came down in a hollow, either to drink or hide from us. When within about 200 yards, he discovered us, and after taking a most deliberate survey of our numbers, and seeming to weigh the chances like a general, he finally took to his heels, and we in hot pursuit. After running about half a mile, Captain Gantt came up and fired two pistols, which took effect in his fore shoulder. By this time I came up, and fired a rifle, the ball of which struck him in the small of the back and passed under his back bone, after which a Cherokee Indian fired a pistol and carbine. By this time he received seven balls, from pistols, principally, and I was ready with my rifle loaded for another shot, but Captain Gantt advised me not to fire, as he would soon die. He had now stopped, and soon began to reel, and fell. He proved to be one of the male kind, about eight years old. We soon flayed him and packed our horses and started for the company, which we overtook in about five miles, all highly satisfied with our exploit. Trailed about ten miles and encamped at a small grove of timber south of the trail and one and a half miles north of Blue River. I have been more minute in describing this day's travel in consequence of its having been the first time buffalo have been seen on the tramp and that merely by accident, as he was probably one who had wandered off from the rest of some drove, as he was the only one seen in the neighborhood, and very poor at that. I mounted as sergeant of the guard for the first time on the trip and had a pleasant night, and had the pleasure of being up to see it all.

"Tuesday, June 13. - I left camp this morning with James Williams and Ed Otey, all mounted on mules, and armed with four pistols, a rifle and a bowie knife each, for the propose of taking a buffalo hunt. We came to Blue River, made a raft, on which we placed our saddles, blankets, guns, pistols, and clothes, then swam over by the raft, and went back and swam the mules. Packed up and took out on the prairie to the dividing ridge between the Republican fork of the Kansas and Blue River, traveled up the ridge

about ten miles, and came onto Blue River and camped at night. Saw no buffalo. Saw five elk and one Indian. Williams shot at one of the elk and missed it. Mister Indian ran off like the devil, leading two horses and riding another.

"Wednesday, June 14. - We went up the Blue River about two miles and swam over in the morning, and met the company about noon, when we learned, greatly to our astonishment, that we had killed two buffalo the day before. One man saw us shoot, and saw the buffalo fall, and got Mr. Burnett and went with him and their horses, and swam Blue River to get some of the meat, but, to their astonishment, they could find neither us nor the meat. So much for the camp story, the origin of which was that we had shot two loads out of our guns, which had been loaded some time. This man saw from the opposite side of the river and made up the buffalo. Camped at night with the company on the bank of Blue River, after traveling sixteen miles today, and ten yesterday. The night we hunters camped at Blue River, the company camped at Ash Creek.

"Thursday, June 15. - Traveled about sixteen miles. Camped on the bank of Blue River. I traveled with the advance guard. I saw several antelope, one killed by a man of our company. Tonight the council assembled to settle some difficulty between John B. Howell and Elbridge Edson. Circumstances too numerous to mention. Weather fine, a little rain at night.

"Friday, June 16. - I traveled with the advance guard. Men hunting in every direction, and killed but little game. Company traveled about eighteen miles and camped on the bank of Blue River. I mount guard. Weather fine and cool.

"Saturday, June 17. - I traveled with the pilot and advance guard. Crossed some small creeks where the mountain road leaves the river. Camped at night, after traveling sixteen miles, at the last timber on Blue River. Weather in the forenoon, rainy; afternoon, clear and fine. Several Pawnees came into camp this evening for the first time. Mr. Applegate's company passed us in the evening. Sergeant Ford on guard.

"Sunday, June 18. - Left the encampment on the waters of the Blue River, and took the upper road across the divide to the River Platte, distance about twenty miles; direction, about northwest. Crossed several Pawnee trails, but not so numerous as some days previous. Struck up the Platte at Grand Island, not far from the head. River very high, appearance muddy, similar to that of the Missouri. Prairie today tolerably level and of a sandy quality. Passed no running water. Some ponds in the prairie. Passed no timber today, nor found any that could be got at the river.

"Monday, June 19. - Started early in the morning, after passing a night without wood. Went about five miles and got breakfast. Encamped at night near the bank of the Platte, after traveling ten miles.

"Tuesday, June 20. - This morning myself and twenty other men started ahead of the company with horses and mules to hunt and pack skins and buffalo meat to the crossing up the South Fork by the time the company should arrive that point. Encamped at night at a small creek called Ash Creek.

"Wednesday, June 21. - Traveled up the Platte River till evening. Killed a buffalo bull and calf, and two antelope, and suffered very much from a very hard, cold rain. Waded a slough and camped on the river bank among some willows. Lay in wet blankets on the wet sand. Extremely cold.

"Thursday, June 22. - Trailed about sixteen miles and camped on the bank of the river. Plenty of good wood and water, and for that reason called it Camp Satisfaction, and the place where we camped the night before Camp Disagreeable.

"Friday, June 23 - Found buffalo about 2:00 o'clock, and killed four, and encamped on the bank of a slough putting into the river. Tonight lived high, had fine times.

"Saturday, June 24. - Laid by all day. I stopped in camp with Mr. Reading and three other men. Dried meat all day. The rest of the men hunted and packed in without much success. Tonight our hunters saw the company encamped four miles in our rear. I stood a tour of guard.

"Sunday, June 25. - Nine of us pushed on to near the crossing and camped at night. The rest went to the company. Formed our camp where the bluffs first come to the river, about six or eight miles below the usual crossing place.

"Monday, June 26. - The company came up and overtook us about noon at the crossing, but found the water so high that it was impossible to ford the river. Traveled about sixteen miles today and camped on the river bank. Burned buffalo wood, as we have done for the last four days. Applegate's company four miles in our rear. General McCarver left us to join the other company.

"Tuesday, June 27. - Traveled about twelve miles. Camped on the bank. At noon five buffalos crossed the river and ran close to the wagons. The Invincibles turned out and kept up a running fire, like a military muster. Succeeded in killing three.

"Wednesday, June 28. - I went ahead with the pilot. At noon we went out about six miles from the river. Saw several buffalo. Killed one old bull, too poor to eat. Brought in his tongue. Camped at night on the bank of

the Platte, after traveling fifteen miles. Weather fine, no rain since the twenty-first of the month. Yesterday we experienced in the morning about 8:00 o'clock a very warm wind from the south and southwest, which lasted about half an hour. Never experienced the like before. I am for guard tonight.

"Thursday, June 29. - Spent some time in the morning attempting to find a fording place in the river, but was unsuccessful in the attempt. Started about 9:00 o'clock. Stopped to eat at 10:00 o'clock near a small pond in the prairie. The water in taste resembled a strong solution of salts, which rendered it unfit for use, in fact, all the water we have had except river water since we struck the Platte has been strongly impregnated with some mineral which is said to be salts and appears to have the effects of that medicine on the person who makes use of it. The ground in many places which are rather low is covered with a white substance which has a salty taste. Captain Gantt calls it sulphate of soda. Traveled today about ten miles and encamped at a grove consisting of some large cottonwood trees, where we intend crossing the river. Sergeant Ford to guard.

"Friday, June 30. - Today laid at grove making arrangements preparatory to crossing. Killed several buffalo. Packed in the skins of eight that were killed last evening to make skin boats.... Camped in the timber at the same place we camped the night before, not moving our wagons. Sergeant Gilmore on guard.

"Saturday, July 1. - Come stir in camp this morning in consequence of a sentinel's gun going off accidentally, which killed a mule belonging to James Williams, the bullet breaking the mule's neck. This is the most serious accident which had yet occurred from carelessness in the use of firearms, though, judging from the carelessness of the men, I have anticipated more serious accidents before this time, and if they do not occur, they will be avoided by great good luck, not by precaution. In the afternoon the company crossed several loads in wagon bodies, which they have covered with raw buffalo hides to prevent their leaking. Captain Applegate and Dr. Whitman came into camp this evening, their company being camped eight miles below this place. Mr. Stewart had the gratification of being presented with a daughter this evening. Weather cool and pleasant.

"Sunday, July 2. - Wind cold and strong from southwest. Our company commence crossing tolerably early. Weather extremely cold and water still colder. Part of the company crossed the river, and the balance lay at Sleepy Grove. My time for guard tonight. Mr. Childs and Waldo joined us this evening, destination, California.

"Monday, July 3. - Continued crossing the river. Two

men arrived in our camp this evening from Applegate's company, to get our skin boats for their company to cross eight miles below this place. They bring us intelligence of one of their company being lost by the name of Bennett O'Neil. He had been out three days. They have made vigilant search which proved unsuccessful. An accident occurred today in our company. Mr. Kerritook, a half-blood Cherokee, went out in the hills in quest of game. In firing at an antelope, his rifle burst at the breech and injured him severely, though not dangerously. Most of our company have crossed with their baggage, their wagons still remaining on the south side. I stopped all night on the south side with a small detachment of our company. Weather fine and cool.

"Tuesday, July 4. - The glorious Fourth has once more rolled around. Myself, with most of our company, celebrated it by swimming and fording the south fork of the Big Platte, with cattle, wagons, baggage and so forth. All this at Sleepy Grove. However, there seems to be some of our company ruminating upon the luxuries destroyed in different parts of the great Republic on this day. Occasionally you hear something said about mint juleps, soda, ice cream, cognac, porter, ale and sherry wine, but the Oregon emigrant must forget those luxuries and, for a time, submit to hard fare, and put up with truly cold-water celebrations, such as we have enjoyed today, namely, drinking cold water and wading and swimming in it all day. This ought to satisfy any cold-water man. If it won't, he must go on to a larger stream than the Big Platte.

"Wednesday, July 5. - About twenty of us go down below camp in the evening, and haul some wagons out of the river which have been left there since yesterday. Company variously engaged, some bringing over their wagons, others packing their goods, preparatory to starting. Weather extremely warm and sultry.

"Remarks. - Sleep Grove. In calculating the distance on our route, we find it 460 miles from Independence. This grove is the first timber of any consequence on the river above where we struck it. The grove consists of large cottonwoods and willows, situated under the bluff on the margin of the river, which is about half a mile wide at this place, and partakes very much of the character of the Missouri River, being full of floating sand, with quicksand beaches, the general direction varying a little from east and west. Finished crossing everything belonging to the company this evening without any serious disaster. After dark we took a little recreation on a sand beach, in the shape of a dance, having two good violin players with their instruments. But that part of the company which is generally most interesting on such occasions, happened to be absent from our party, viz: the ladies. This deficiency was not owning to there being none with the caravan, as we have several bright-eyed girls along, but we deemed it rather unnecessary to invite them to participate in our rough exercise of kicking sand.

"Thursday, July 6. - The whole company went seven miles down the river to get timber. Encamped all night on the bank. Killed one buffalo. Childs and Waldo's company left us here and went on three miles further. Several wagons broke off from our company to join them, among the rest, Old Prairie Chicken. Nobody sorry. I mount guard as sergeant. Rained in the night.

"Friday, July 7. - Crossed the divide between the two forks of the Platte, course about north, northwest. Traveled twenty-five miles. Camped on the north fork about two miles in the rear of Childs and Waldo. Several of our men lost this evening. A little rain in the night.

"Saturday, July 8. - The company traveled up the north fork about eighteen miles. Myself and three others went back on the plains to hunt some lost men belonging to our company. Found them in about seven miles and overtook the company at noon. Roads in some places rather sandy. Saw no buffalo today except a few on the north side of the river.

"Sunday, July 9. - Traveled about fifteen miles, and camped on the bank of the river. Came in sight of the Chimney about noon. Childs and Waldo's company still ahead. I mount sergeant of the guard and have some sport. Gave two members of the old guard a tour by way of punishment for sleeping on post the night before. Found one of my men sleeping at post and took his gun away from him.

"Monday, July 10. - Childs and Waldo out of sight ahead. I go on with a party to look at the Chimney. Eight or ten of us ascend to the top of the mound from whence the shaft or column of clay and sand ascends abut 150 feet above the mound, which is about 200 feet high, making 350 feet above the level of the plains, and one of the greatest curiosities I have ever seen in the west, and can be seen distinctly thirty miles on the plains. The shaft is about twenty-five feet in diameter, and at a distance of thirty miles, resembles the trunk of a tree standing erect. There are also many other mounds and high clay bluffs in the neighborhood of the Chimney. We camped at night in the bank of the Platte about nine miles from the Chimney. Its appearance from here resembles a funnel reversed. Traveled sixteen miles today.

"Tuesday, July 11. - Company left the Platte this morning and turned to the left in order to avoid some high bluffs on the river. Mr. Reading and myself left the trail and kept between it and the river, in order to examine the curiosities in the hills. Passed some very high bluffs, one of which we named the Betzar, in consequence of its resembling a building of that name in Cincinnati. We went down some very deep ravines, some of which were fifty feet, with perpendicular banks, in some places only wide enough for a mule to pass. We killed one badger and shot at two buffalo. We struck the company at 4:00 o'clock and camped on a small creek in the prairie, about four miles from the river. At this place we got a view of the Black Hills, 100 miles distant. Company today traveled twenty miles. Weather warm.

"Wednesday, July 12. - Sold a gun at camp this morning, belonging to Isaac Williams, for having gone to sleep on post last night. In traveling ten miles we struck a sandy creek, and the river in four miles after. Camped on the bank of the river, under some high, sandy and clay bluffs, after traveling sixteen miles. I mounted sergeant of the guard.

"Thursday, July 13. - Traveled about twelve miles. Passed an old fort about 2:00 o'clock on the banks of the river. The ground we have traveled over today seems to partake of a more undulating character. This evening our advance guard returned over the hills bringing information that there was an Indian village about two miles in advance, probably Sioux. We deemed it expedient to turn over to the right and encamp on the river, rather than camp in the neighborhood of the village. The boys seemed to be busily engaged in scouring up their old rifles and making other arrangements preparatory for Indian fighting, although we anticipate no danger.

"Friday, July 14. - Arrived at Fort Laramie about 10:00 o'clock where we found Childs and Applegate's company. Found Laramie Ford very high, and the company was engaged all the afternoon and all night in ferrying. The boys at Fort Platte gave us a ball in the evening, where we received hospitable treatment.

"Saturday, July 15. - The company finished crossing this morning. We lay here today making some arrangements for starting. Saw some of the Sioux Indians who had come in from the recent fight with Pawnees on the forks of the Platte, where they killed thirty-six, six or seven only escaping. I swapped guns twice today and got the worst of the bargain.

"Sunday, July 16. - The company got under way this morning, traveling out to the big spring on Sand Creek, about eight miles, in company with Childs. Camped together, Applegate's company having gone ahead. We camped at the spring all night. Ford on guard.

"Monday, July 17. - Traveled about sixteen miles, country very rough and hills very high. Camped at night between the two canyons of the Platte.

"Tuesday, July 18. - Childs' company traveled ahead. Stopped at noon, just below a canyon on the Platte. Camped at night at a dry creek with a great deal of cottonwood. Traveled fifteen miles. Made camp in the point between the Platte and the cottonwoods. Very high bluffs on the opposite side.

"Wednesday, July 19. - Country very rough, it being the worst part of the Black Hills. Passed some red bluffs, and in some places red pulverized earth, resembling vermillion, covered the ground. Traveled about twenty miles. Camped on Big Rock Creek, having passed Deer Creek during the day. Ford on guard. An alarm at night originated in some very smart young men firing their guns near the camp after dark, and for so doing were put under guard by order of Colonel Martin. They raised a row with the guard, and like to have made a serious matter of it, and as it was, they cocked their rifles and threatened to shoot.

"Thursday, July 20. - I came on ahead with Captain Gantt and an advance guard, passed over some very rough road, and at noon came up to a fresh grave with stones piled over it, and a note tied on a stick, informing us that it was the grave of Joel Hembree, child of Joel J. Hembree, aged six years, and was killed by a wagon running over its body. At the head of the grave stood a stone containing the name of the child, the first death that has occurred on the expedition. The grave is on the left hand side of the trail, close to Squaw Butte Creek. After crossing the creek we came to a party of mountaineers from the Black's Fork of Green River. They had stopped for dinner. Had several pack horses packed with furs belonging to Mr. Vasques, who treated us very hospitably. We found with Mr. Vasques and his party, two men returning from Oregon, giving a very bad account of that country. They also had letters to some of our company, which differed very much from their verbal account. We traveled today about twelve miles. Childs' company of five wagons left our company and went on to the crossing of North Fork.

"Friday, July 21. - Left Squaw Butte Creek, traveled fifteen miles and camped on the Platte. I mount as sergeant of the guard.

"Saturday, July 22. - Trailed six miles and camped on the platte about noon, and endeavored to find a ford. Several men sick in camp, afflicted with a kind of fever. The company discontented and strong symptoms of mutiny. Some anxious to travel faster, some slower, some want to cross the river here, some want to go ahead, and others want to go any way but the right way. This will always be the difficulty with heterogeneous masses of emigrants crossing these plains. While every man's will is his law, and lets him act or do as he pleases, he will always find friends to support him. In order to obviate this difficulty and maintain good order in large companies, the presence of military force, and a declaration of martial law is highly necessary. Then emigrants will travel in peace, harmony and good order. They have the elements of their own destruction within themselves.

"Sunday, July 23. This is my birthday, being twenty-three years of age, and upwards of 3,000 miles west of the place of my birth. The company got under way. Edwin Otey and myself struck out toward a large mountain south in quest of game. I shot an antelope and returned to the company about noon. Found them nooning on the ground near the ford, where Applegate's company had crossed the river the evening previous. We came in sight of them about 3:00 o'clock crossing a high ridge at right angles with the river. Two men from Childs' company met us this evening, informing us that they were all across the north fork, about ten miles ahead, but could not find Sir William Stewart's gum elastic boat, as they had directions they would find it in the fork of a tree. Elected five councilmen. Traveled twelve miles. Camped on a small creek about a mile from the Platte. Sergeant Gilmore for guard.

"Monday, July 24. - Got up to the crossing about noon. Applegate's company on the opposite side. Drove across in the afternoon without difficulty. Camped at night on the banks of the platte. Traveled six miles. I mount guard.

"Tuesday, July 25. - Left the Platte, struck across to Sweetwater, trailed about eighteen miles and camped on a salt creek.

"Wednesday, July 26. - Company started on a buffalo hunt under the direction of Captain Gantt. Saw a great many buffalo. Captain Gantt got mad and all separated. I killed a buffalo. Overtook the company at night, they having trailed eighteen miles. Company camped on a beautiful creek seven miles from Sweetwater.

"Thursday, July 27. - Six of us started on a buffalo hunt this morning, crossing a mountain, killed three cows and several bulls. Camped out all night; lay without blankets or coats in the rain. Company consisted of Edwin and Morris Otey, Chimp, Jackson, Howell and myself. Saw a great many buffalo and had a severe night without sleeping. Company traveled eight miles.

"Friday, July 28. - Looked around camp this morning; found the buffalo all traveling. Probably got wind of the caravan. Started for the company about 8:00 o'clock in a very cold rain. Howell took sick and threw away his meat. Got up to our wagons in the evening. They lay at Independence Rock, our company having split. Colonel Martin, with most of the wagons, has gone ahead. Our

wagon and some others of his company fell in with some deserters from Applegate's company, making in all nineteen wagons. All the rest of the company ahead. Applegate's camp on Sweetwater at the rock, and our company just below. The Oregon emigrating company has been strangely divided, and no doubt the division will be again divided. The material it is formed of can not be controlled.

"Saturday, July 29. - Applegate's company leaves the rock this morning. Our little company remains at its first camp. Captain Cooper assumes command of the company. We spend the day in drying meat, cleaning up our wet firearms, making moccasins, etc. Several of our men are out hunting; others came in this evening, and report that the buffalo are all on the move in the direction of the Yellowstone River. Some hunters arrive at our camp tonight, who belong to the other company, bringing but little meat. I mount guard as private tonight for the first time on the trip.

"Sunday, July 30. - Most beautiful morning, the weather calm and serene. After breakfast, myself, with some other young men, had the pleasure of waiting on five or six young ladies to pay a visit to Independence Rock. I had the satisfaction of putting the names of Miss Mary Zachary and Miss Jane Mills on the southeast point of the rock, near the road, on a high point. Facing the road, in all the splendor of gunpowder, tar and buffalo grease, may be seen the name of J. W. Nesmith, from Maine, with an anchor. Above it on the rock may be found the names of trappers, emigrants, and gentlemen of amusement, some of which have been written these ten years. The rock is an unshappen pile, about half a mile long, and half that breadth, and 100 feet high, and is accessible at three or four places. The composition of the rock I am unable to give geologically, but its appearance is a flinty, gray substance, mixed with limestone and very hard. Sweet Water River runs by the foot of it about fifty yards distant, and a great many high mountains and peaks are in the neighborhood. The distance from Sweet Water to Platte by road is about forty-three miles. Wood and water scarce. Plenty of salt water and mountain sage and chamisso (a small evergreen shrub), which answers as a substitute for wood. In fact, salt lakes and salt springs may be found all through this country.

"Monday, July 31. - Left the encampment near Independence Rock about 11:00 o'clock. Came up to Martin's company about 1:00 o'clock and found some very sick men in the company. Among the rest were Mr. Payne and Stevenson. The latter seemed very dangerous of fever, and flighty, uttering incoherent sentences. His situation excited my sympathy, to see a fine, stout young man reduced to a wreck by disease, far from his home and friends. I took a parting look, never expecting to behold him again. We went three miles beyond Martin's company and camped, trailed seven miles. We have in company thirteen wagons and thirty-one men, a small band, indeed, but all seemed determined to go on through. We camped on Sweetwater, with a high range of mountains on the right, or northwest, the mountains composed principally of solid rock. Applegate and Childs ahead. Old Zachary, a man fond of rows, has been excluded from Martin's company for defrauding a young man by the name of Matney out of his provisions, and throwing him off in the wilderness. The old rogue, with the two Oteys, is encamped about a mile ahead alone; a small camp, but a big rascal. Visited the Canyon of the Sweetwater. The cut is in a rock about eight feet wide and 200 feet high.

"Tuesday, August 1. - Traveled twenty miles. I went hunting with three others, killed a bull. Vasques and Walker's mountain party came up with us. We all camped close to Child's company at Sweet Water under a point of mountain. Twenty miles.

"Wednesday, August 2. - Childs and Walker left us this morning, turning to the left for the purpose of curing meat. I went out with Captain Applegate and Dr. Whitman and took dinner at their encampment, on a sand creek, where they had killed seven cows the evening previous. All hands considerably alarmed about Indians, fearing an attack from the Cheyennes and Sioux, who are said to be in camp in great numbers forty miles south on the Platte, I returned having trailed seven miles today. Martin's company close in the rear. Came in sight of a high range of mountains with snow on them, said to be the Mountains of Wind River. Martin's company passed us and encamped a mile and a half ahead.

"Thursday, August 3. - Made an early start; passed Martin's company in corral. Left Sweetwater to the right and made a cut-off of the bend. Traveled eighteen miles before we struck the river; found only a little water in one place, which was strongly impregnated with sulphur. The country presents a barren aspect, very sandy, and covered with sage. Mountains in every direction in sight. Encamped at night where we struck the river. Trailed twenty miles. Martin's company camped on the river 200 yards below our encampment. I mount guard; fourth relief.

"Friday, August 4. - Mr Payne, a man in Martin's company, died this morning at 3:00 o'clock. He suffered severely, being unwell since we left Fort Laramie. Died of inflammation of the bowels, leaving a wife and four small children. He was decently interred on a rise of ground at

the left of the road. Myself, with four others, went hunting and killed no game. About 2:00 o'clock in the afternoon we heard a loud, sharp report, seeming to be in the air directly above us, and resembling the report of a piece of heavy artillery. After the first report, there was a loud rumbling sound overhead. I never heard the like before, though such reports are said to be frequent in the mountains. At the time of hearing the noise, there were no clouds to be seen of any size. We came up to our company encamped on Sweetwater, in the evening, having traveled ten miles.

"Saturday, August 5. - Traveled fifteen miles over very rough road. Several of us went hunting, killed one antelope, one groundhog and five sage hens. Crossed several small branches of good water. High mountains in sight. Nights very cold; middle of the day very warm. Trailed eighteen miles. Distance to Fort Laramie, 231 miles.

"Sunday, August 6. - Traveled twelve miles. Passed Applegate's company and encamped on Sweetwater. Wind River Mountains in sight.

"Monday, August 7. - Left Sweetwater this morning, it being the last water of the Atlantic that we see. Traveled six miles and nooned at the spring. In the afternoon, struck out across the twenty-mile barren, without wood, water or grass. Stopped half way, having traveled sixteen miles. Crossed the Divide August 7.

"Tuesday, August 8. - After a considerable delay, in consequence of the cattle wandering off in quest of food, we gathered up and left camp about 9:00 o'clock. Traveled until about 2:00 o'clock a.m., across a plain of sand and sage, and encamped on Sandy, a small tributary of the Colorado We now consider ourselves in Oregon Territory, and we consider this part of it, a poor sample of the El Dorado. We encamped on Sandy, Applegate's and Martin's company having gone ahead. Traveled ten miles.

"Wednesday, August 9. - I started on ahead to go to Fort Bridger, but stopped at Ham's Fork, and most of our company and men arrived at Fort Bridger, on Black's Ford, Monday, August 14.

"Tuesday, August 15. - Cooper puts up his tools and does some work for the company. I will here remark, as I have not kept the separate day's travel and distances, that from Little Sandy to here the distance is sixty miles. On those days which I have neglected journalizing, there was nothing of importance occurred, except the death of Mr. Stevenson, which took place on August 9. He was buried on the banks of Big Sandy.

"Wednesday, August 16. - Remained all day at the fort. Cooper trades his large wagon and the blacksmith's tools for a smaller one. A child of Mr. Carey's died yesterday

18

and was buried this morning.

"Tuesday, August 17. - Left the fort this morning, all the rest of the wagons having previously started. We struck out for Muddy Creek, where we arrived about noon, and proceeded up the creek about eight miles, making, in all, twenty miles travel today. This is the most barren country I have seen yet, as it is entirely destitute of grass, excepting occasionally a very little along the creek. In the evening, as we attempted to cross Muddy, our large wagon capsized, throwing all the loading into the water and wet all our clothing, blankets also. Our flour we saved without any material injury. After an hour's wading in water and mud waist deep, we succeeded in getting everything out, excepting the coupling pole broke. We replaced it with a new one after dark. Traveled twenty miles.

"Friday, August 18. - Traveled twelve miles; overtook Waldo's company on the head of Muddy Creek.

"Saturday, August 19. - Left the head of Muddy this morning. Crossed a large mountain. Found some of the cattle absent; myself and Major Hall went back in quest of them, but we ascertained at Stoughton's camp that they were driven ahead. We rode until midnight over very rough road before we overtook the company. Traveled fifteen miles.

"Sunday, August 20. - Struck Bear River about noon, and traveled down it about ten miles over a fine level bottom. Course, Northwest. Traveled about twenty miles.

"Monday, August 21. - Traveled twenty miles down Bear River and camped on the bank. Upset McHaley's wagon in Bear River.

"Tuesday, August 22. - Seven wagons of us left camp this morning, leaving McHaley and Applegate to lay by. We leave the river and cross over a high mountain about three miles and come to the river at night. Traveled fifteen miles. Encamped on the river; caught some fine, large trout and chubs. Traveled eighteen miles.

"Wednesday, August 23. - Lieutenant Freemont, of the U. S. Topographical Engineers, with his party, overtook us this morning. Myself and Mr. Otey go on ahead to get an ox of ours in the other company. Came up to a village of Snake Indians at noon. Did some trading. I bought a black horse. Traveled fifteen miles.

Thursday, August 24. - Passed the Soda Springs about 2:00 o'clock. Camped on Bear River at a place where our trail leaves it. Trailed eighteen miles.

"Friday, August 25. - Leave Bear River; traveled twenty miles over to a creek running into the Snake River, by the name of Portneuf. Saw today signs of volcanic eruptions. They appear to be numerous all along Bear River. The stones which lay about large sinks in the ground, have the appearance of melted clay, and ring like earthenware. Their appearance is very singular. However, the greatest curiosity in this part of the country are the soda springs, which boil up in level ground and sink again. They are quite numerous and have exactly the taste of soda water without the syrup. The springs are continually sparkling and foaming. Camped on Portneuf.

"Saturday, August 26 - Trailed sixteen miles; camped at some springs. Kit Carson, of Freemont's company, camped with us, on his return from Fort Hall, having been on express.

"Sunday, August 27. - Trailed twenty miles and camped to the left of the trail, near where we strike off for Snake River. Most of the country is very rough that we have passed today.

"Monday, August 28. - Trailed twelve miles today and arrived at Fort Hall, where we remained until Friday, September 1. Here the company had considerable trading with Grant, manager here for the Hudson's Bay Company. He sells at an exorbitant price; flour, 25 cents per pint; sugar, 50; coffee, 50; rice, 33 1-3. Part of the company went on with pack animals, leaving their wagons. Nothing of importance occurred, with the exception of a Mr. Richardson dying. Was buried August 31 at Fort Hall.

"Friday, September 1. - Got under way this morning. Weather very cold and rainy, as it has been for the last three days. Trailed down Snake River fifteen miles. Passed some fine mill sites. Camped on Snake River.

"Saturday, September 2. - Road very rough today. Broke our wagon tongue. Trailed eighteen miles. Camped on a small branch about six miles from the river.

"Sunday, September 3. - This morning Jackson, Cooper's teamster, left and joined Zachary's mess. Trailed sixteen miles without wood, water or grass. Camped on a small branch with excellent grass.

"Monday, September 4. - Got an early start this morning. Traveled ten miles to the river. Nooned on the river. Traveled down it and camped on the bank, making twenty miles today. The river here assumes a broad, placid, and beautiful appearance, the water being very clear, unlike any of the rivers in the Western states.

"Tuesday, September 5. - Traveled twelve miles. Encamped on the bank of a creek, with but little water, and that in holes. Stopped about 2:00 o'clock and lay by in the afternoon, as it was raining. Two lodges of Nez Perces Indians, returning to Walla Walla from Fort Hall.

"Wednesday, September 6. - Trailed eight miles and struck Rock Creek. Trailed eight down it. Encamped in the canyon at the crossing, making sixteen miles trailed. Rainy in the evening.

"Thursday, September 7. - Left the canyon in the morning and traveled twenty miles over a country destitute of grass. Struck the river ten miles above the Salmon Falls. Encamped for the night. Trailed twenty miles.

"Friday, September 8. - Trailed down five miles. Encamped on a creek with good grass. I went down to the falls and purchased some fine salmon. Had a fight in camp this evening. Old Zachary stabbed Mr. Wheeler with his knife.

"Saturday, September 9. - Passed the falls and trailed twenty miles. Encamped on a big bluff without grass. White's ox fell down the bluff and broke his neck.

"Sunday, September 10. - I took a trip down the river this morning in quest of animals. Overtook the wagons in two miles. Traveled eight miles. Encamped on an island in the river.

"Monday, September 11. - Crossed the river this morning without difficulty. Trailed four miles. Encamped on a dry branch, water in holes.

"Tuesday, September 12. - We were detained in camp this morning until 12:00 o'clock in consequence of an ox running off. Trailed five miles in the afternoon. Encamped on a small creek. Grass tolerable.

"Wednesday, September 13. - Trailed fifteen miles. Passed the Hot Spring about noon. Water almost boiling. Camped on a small branch.

"Thursday, September 14. - Traveled eight miles and lay by at a small creek in the afternoon. Weather fine.

"Friday, September 15. - Lost my horse this morning, and trailed a-foot all day. Found my horse at camp, Cooper having brought him on and left me to walk all day. We traveled twenty miles. Country very rough. Camped on a small branch, eight miles west of the deep hole spring.

"Saturday, September 16. - Trailed eighteen miles today, the country not quite so rough as we have had. Very little stone or sage. Encamped at night on Boise River.

"Sunday, September 17. - Trailed down Boise on the south side. Traveled sixteen miles. Encamped on the bank of the river. Indians in camp this evening. We have seen them for the last four or five days. Every day they come to sell us dried salmon, and present a poor, squalid appearance, besides being d--d lousy.

"Monday, September 18. - Trailed ten miles down the river and crossed. Trailed three miles down the north side and encamped early, making thirteen miles trailed today. Find the grass tolerably good on Boise River.

"Tuesday, September 19. - Haggard and myself went to Fort Boise ahead of the wagons; distance ten miles. The wagons arrived in the afternoon. The wind blowing very hard from the northwest, we found it impossible to ford the river, as the swells rolled very high. Encamped for the night just below the fort. Visited Monsieur Payette, the commandant; found him a very agreeable old French gentleman, and has been in this country, in the fur trade, since 1810, having left New York in that year and came around by sea to the mouth of the Columbia, in the employment of Mr. Astor. We spent a pleasant evening in his company and had a dance.

"Wednesday, September 20. - Crossed the river this afternoon without any difficulty, water being about four feet six inches deep. Encamped on the south side of the river.

"Thursday, September 21. - Left the river this morning. Traveled twelve miles and encamped on a creek called Malheur. Warm spring on the bank.

"Friday, September 22. - Trailed seventeen miles and encamped on a small stream. Country very rough.

"Saturday, September 23. - Trailed five miles and struck Snake River; said to be the last sight we get of it. Trailed four miles and struck Burnt River, making nine miles. Killed a beef in the evening. Provisions getting scarce.

"Sunday, September 24. - Trailed ten miles over the roughest country I ever saw, Burnt River being hemmed in by hills on both sides. Encamped in the bottom.

"Monday, September 25. - Trailed eight miles. Passed the forks of Burnt River. The roads rough and the country rougher still. Encamped near the head of the left hand fork of Burnt River. In the forenoon passed a fine grove of large timber, principally Balm of Gilead, close by a patch of fine black haws, which we devoured most voraciously.

"Tuesday, September 26. - Trailed ten miles. Passed another fork of Burnt River, with an Indian village close by. Encamped at a place where the trail leaves Burnt River near the spring.

"Wednesday, September 27. - Looney's wagon turned over this morning soon after leaving camp. We crossed the divide and encamped at the lone pine tree. Trailed twelve miles. Snow, that fell the night before last on the mountains in sight all day. Weather drizzly and rainy.

"Thursday, September 28. - Left the pine tree this morning. Trailed fourteen miles. Encamped on the third fork of Powder River. Had a fine view of the snow-topped mountains through the clouds. Raining below them.

"Friday, September 29. - Trailed sixteen miles and encamped in Grande Ronde, beautiful bottom prairie about six miles across and surrounded by mountains capped with snow. Had some difficulty in entering the Ronde in consequence of the big hill which it was necessary for us to descend. Soil today assumed a more fertile appearance than any I have seen west of the mountains, in some places covered with beautiful green grass, giving it the appearance of spring.

"Saturday, September 30. - Trailed six miles across Grande Ronde. Encamped at the foot of the mountains, and lay by in the afternoon.

"Sunday, October 1. - Started over the mountains. Trailed twelve miles and encamped on a small dry creek in a deep ravine. Today E. Otey and myself went hunting. Had a beautiful prospect of the Grande Ronde from the top of the mountains. Found the mountains covered with evergreen trees which remind me of the scenes of my childhood. They consists of pine, spruce, hemlock, fir, and tamarack or juniper. Mrs. Rubey died at Grande Ronde, and was buried October 1.

"Monday, October 2. - Trailed twelve miles today over bad roads, in many places timber to be cut. I went in advance and cut timber all day. Encamped at night on a small stream of good water.

"Tuesday, October 3. - Had some difficulty this morning in finding our oxen, some of them having lain down in the pine thickets. Started about ten o'clock. Trailed about three miles. Crossed a very bad ravine and encamped on the west side of it. Weather since we left Grande Ronde fine, warm and mild. Nights rather cool.

"Wednesday, October 4. - Weather stormy; rain and hail. We got under way and traveled twelve miles down the west side of the Blue Mountains, when we struck the Umatilla River. Went three miles down it, and encamped near some Cayuse lodges. Cooper had the fore axle-tree of his wagon broken off this evening by two Indian bulls charging on the team, and causing them to run around. McDaniel, the driver, shot at one of them with a pistol, wounding him in the mouth.

"Thursday, October 5. - Delayed some time in camp this morning in hunting cattle and horses, many of the later having wandered off and the Indian horses being so numerous made it difficult for us to find our own. Started about noon on the trail for Dr. Whitman's. Traveled eight miles and encamped for the night. Sticcas, a very friendly Indian who piloted us across the Blue Mountains, accompanied us today and camped with us tonight.

"Friday, October 6. - This morning I joined with Otey and Haggard and went on with the carriages to Dr. Whitman's, where we arrived about two o'clock. We purchased one bushel of potatoes and a peck of corn, they having no flour. Traveled on four miles toward Walla Walla. Encamped before night close to the creek, making twenty miles today. Weather rainy and misty until evening, when the sun came out.

"Saturday, October 7. - Left camp early this morning and followed down the Walla Walla until 3 o'clock, when we encamped for the night. I purchased some roots today from an Indian, which they call kamash. It is a small root of oval form and of a dark color, has a very sweet taste. The Indian made bread of it, which is very palatable. A few Cayuse Indians encamped close by us, of whom we purchased some corn and potatoes, and they in return, stole a tin cup from us. They possess great faculties for business of this sort.

"Sunday, October 8. - Left our Cayuse neighbors this morning in good season and started for Fort Walla Walla, where we arrived in three hours. It is situated at the mouth of the Walla Walla River, from which it takes its name. It commands a view of the Columbia River, otherwise the prospect is dreary. Above and below are high bluffs, while near to the fort are sand banks not possessing fertility enough to sprout a pea, and in fact this is too much the case with all the far-famed Walla Walla Valley. There are some spots of good soil immediately on the streams, but from Dr. Whitman's to the fort, a distance of twenty-four miles, there is no timber except a little cottonwood, or a species of Balm of Gilead, and at the fort there is not a tree in sight on either side of the Columbia River. If this is a fair specimen of Oregon, it falls far below the conceptions which I formed of the country. At the fort we could procure no eatables. Could only get a little tobacco, and Mr. McKinley, the manager, was loth to part with that, in consequence of its being the Sabbath. The whole country looks poverty stricken. We went two miles below the fort, where we found a little grass and encamped there for the purpose of waiting until Monday to trade.

"Monday, October 9. - This morning E. Otey and myself visited the fort. Bought some tobacco and corn and other small articles. Mr. McKinley visited our camp in the afternoon and we traded him the wagon and harness for a horse, concluding to pack from here on. Made some pack rigs today, and made arrangements for packing. Two Indians camped with us all night. Weather fine.

"Tuesday, October 10. - Took the wagon to the fort this morning and got the horse which we traded for yesterday. Otey and myself made two pack-saddles. Several Indians encamped with us nearly all day, and one young fellow who camped with us last night seems to be inclined to remain, as he is yet in camp. Says he is going to the Methodist Mission, which is 120 miles on our route. Our camp is quite a picturesque place. Immediately under the high bluff of the far-famed Columbia, about one-half mile above are two rocks rising 100 feet above the level of the river. They are separated by small space, and are nearly round, presenting the appearance of two towers. Mr. McKinley informed me that the Indians looked upon them with a great deal of veneration, and say that they are two

Indian damsels, petrified. I must confess that their appearance does not correspond very well with the tradition. Some wagons arrive from Dr. Whitman's this evening. Night very cool.

"Wednesday, October 11. - Mr. Haggard went to the fort this morning to do some trading. After he returned, we packed all our effects on two mules and started about eight o'clock. Travel leisurely until evening down the river a distance of twelve miles. The river varies from one-half to one mile in width, has bars in the middle frequently; the water is quite clear and beautiful. High bluffs on both sides, not a tree in sight all day. Found a little green grass where we encamped at night, near Windmill Rock. Our trail leads immediately under the bluffs. Our Indian still remains with us.

"Thursday, October 12. - Started in good season, traveled all day over a poor, sandy country. Not a tree in sight all day. Met Mr. McDonald and a small party from Fort Vancouver on his way to Fort Hall. He advises us to be on our guard for the Indians, as there are only three of us, and they are very saucy, having three days ago robbed five men of all they had, at the same time drawing their bows and arrows, and threatening to use them if the men did not give up the property. We traveled at least twenty-five miles today and camped a little before sunset, with but little grass for our jaded animals. Our Indian companion, Yeuemah, left us today, crossing the river. We passed some rocky rapids today in several places, but at our camp the river is beautiful, broad, clear, and placid, but the barrenness of the surrounding country affords but a dreary prospect to a man from the Western States. Were the banks of this noble river studded with fine timber and bordered with anything like good soil, its beauty would be unsurpassed. Weather fine.

"Friday, October 13. - Packed up and started about eight o'clock. Traveled down the river over sandy plains. The surrounding country still retains an arid, barren appearance, without timber or grass, but the river in itself is most beautiful. Weather fine. Warm days and cool, moonlight nights. Traveled about twenty miles. Camped early in a little ravine, where there is good grass, and is entirely surrounded by willows, in a quiet retired place, hoping that the Indians will not find us, as their company is anything but agreeable.

"Saturday, October 14. - As we anticipated last night, we had an agreeable night's rest in consequence of the Indians not finding us. Started early and traveled until late, probably twenty-five miles, which is a hard day's ride over this country of sand and stone. A Cayuse Indian brought us some salmon which we purchased, giving him in return some powder and ball. Weather fine.

"Sunday, October 15. - This morning our Indian paid us another visit. We gave him some breakfast, over which, to our astonishment, he asked a blessing in his own tongue. Today we traveled leisurely, crossed a small stream, and passed over some very rugged road, the pack trail in some places going along on the steep and almost perpendicular side of the bluffs 100 feet above the Columbia, and the rock rising 100 feet almost hanging over the trail. In fact, it was rather disagreeable riding along in some places to look down. In event of your horse making a mis-step, himself and rider would be thrown down an awful precipice and buried in the gulf below. Such leaps might suit Sam Patch, but the thought of them is enough for me. We found some good grass and camped early. Traveled about sixteen miles. The river maintains its beauty, in some places interrupted by high rocks rising in its center and strong rapids. Saw a few scrubby trees today. Weather beautifully mild and pleasant.

"Monday, October 16. - In four miles' travel we struck the Deschutes River. Hired two Indians to conduct us across the ford, which we crossed without difficulty. Just below we passed the Dalles, quite a waterfall on the Columbia. Arrived at the Methodist Mission in the evening.

"Tuesday, October 17. - Remained at the Mission all day. Otey and I looked for canoe timber. Weather drizzly.

"Wednesday, October 18. - Ground some wheat in the evening. Some five or six arrived from above. I swapped my horse for a Chinook canoe.

"Thursday, October 19. - Made some arrangements and started about two o'clock with an Indian pilot. Went five miles and camped. Weather fine.

"Friday, October 20. - Paddled down the river all day; scenery wild and romantic. Encamped at night on the north side of the river with some Indians.

"Saturday, October 21. - Made an early start with two Indian canoes in company. Arrived at the Cascades about ten o'clock. Spent the balance of the day in making the portage. On each side of the river at the Cascades are high mountains covered with dead timber, killed by a fire.

"Sunday, October 22. - Got breakfast and started in good season with our pilot and another young Indian. They ran the rapids, which were rough in consequence of wind, and we walked around. Pulled down the river about eight miles and were obliged to encamp in consequence of headwind, which made rather too much swell for our canoe to ride in safety. We encamped on the north side of the river. The boys killed two pheasants. Weather fine and pleasant.

"Monday, October 23. - The wind high this morning from the southeast. Hoisted a sail on our canoe. We all got out to walk around a point while the Indians should run the canoe through, which they did and landed. The other boys missed the trail and kept back in the bluffs. I came to the canoe and waited for them until nearly sundown. Passed off the time in reading Shakespeare's "Merry Wives of Windsor". The wind continued high. I started at an hour by the sun and ran until some time after dark, when I discovered a fire on the north bank of the river, which the Indians said was "Boston Fire," meaning white men. I ran for the fire and fired my pistols, which were soon answered by those at the fire. Upon coming up, I found them to be McDaniel, Haggard, and Otey, who had missed the trail in the morning and having walked twenty miles, concluded to wait for the canoe.

"Tuesday, October 24. - Arrived at the Hudson Bay Company's mill about seven miles above the fort, at twelve o'clock, where we met Waters, Tharp, Marten and Smith, taking up a barge to bring the families down from the Mission. Left the mill and soon arrived at Fort Vancouver, where we found the brigs, Vancouver and Columbia, and also one schooner. We were kindly treated by Dr. McLoughlin, in charge of the fort. Gave us a good dinner and showed us other courtesies. We passed down one mile below the fort and camped for the night.

"Wednesday, October 25. - Took the wrong track. Encamped a little above the mouth of the Willamette.

"Thursday, October 26. - Met the schooner Pallas. Camped on the north side of the Willamette.

"Friday, October 27. - Arrive at Oregon City at the falls of the Willamette.

"Saturday, October 28. - Went to work."

*   *   *

CHAPTER II

The Molalla Indians

Indian Henry
ca. 1913
Dressed in his celebration finery for the arrival of the first train.

Courtesy of the Molalla Historical Society.

Bibliography:

Author Unknown, "Indian Henry," <u>Molalla Pioneer</u>, September 25, 1913
Crawford, Agnes of Molalla, Oregon, Unrecorded Interview, Fall of 1990.
Lynch, Vera Martin, "Indians, including the Klamath and Molalla Tribes," <u>Free Land for Free Men</u>, 1973
Mackey, Harold, "New Light on the Molalla Indians," <u>Oregon Historical Quarterly</u>, March, 1972
Perry, Hazel, "Last Indian Dies as Buckeroo Begins," <u>Molalla Pioneer</u>, June 19, 1972
Stern, Theodore, "The Klamath Indians & the Treaty of 1864," <u>Oregon Historical Quarterly, #57</u>, 1956
Toll, Dale R., "Last of the Molallas," Published Manuscript
Vernon, Stivers, "Saga of the Molalla Hills," <u>The Oregonian</u>, April 29, 1934
Warnock, John, "War on the Abiqua," <u>The Bulletin</u>, November 16, 1983
Zucker, <u>Oregon Indians, Culture, History & Current Affairs</u>, 1983

PART ONE:

"The Last of the Molallas"

by Gail McCormick

The Molalla Indians were a tribe related to the Cayuses, forming the western division of the Cayuse family. The unaware may incorrectly assume that the Molalla Indians roamed only near Molalla, Oregon. However, their relatively small bands roamed the western slopes of the Cascades, from the Clackamas to the Rogue River. And they roamed as far east as the Deschutes River in their seasonal food gathering rounds.

By the time the first wagon train arrived in Oregon City in 1843, except for a few skirmishes, the Molalla's warlike nature was confined to atrocities against other Indian tribes. Upon arrival in south Clackamas County in 1844, settlers William Hatchette Vaughan and Harrison Wright used a friendly strategy to convince the Indians it would be to their advantage to remain friendly with the settlers. Early settlers even purchased their land claims from the Indians. John Dickey, who settled Dickey Prairie, paid the Indians by an exchange of blankets, a gun and other items, totalling $100. The Harrison Wright family employed friendly Indians and the Wright children played often with the Indian children and spoke the Indian jargon fluently. Agnes Crawford, granddaughter of Harrison Wright, tells how to count to fifteen in Indian jargon, as related to her by her father, Reuben Wright, Sr.: (pronounced the way it is spelled)

Number	1:	ix
Number	2:	mox
Number	3:	clone
Number	4:	lockrt
Number	5:	quinum
Number	6:	toofin
Number	7:	cinamox
Number	8:	taha
Number	9:	toe tahu
Number	10:	tosslum
Number	11:	toss a pix
Number	12:	toss a mox
Number	13:	toss a clone
Number	14:	toss a lockrt
Number	15:	toss a quinum
Number	16:	toss a toofin

However, in November of 1847, the news of the Whitman massacre electrified the whole Oregon Territory and put most white settlers on the edge regarding the Indians. When one local troublemaker, by the name of Crooked Finger, sought to start an uprising in the spring of 1848 it was quickly squelched by the white settlers.

Crooked Finger had disappeared late in the year of 1847, traveling to the southern Oregon, to try to get the Klamath Indians to help him drive out the settlers. He succeeded in bringing warriors to the Molalla Prairie but the uprising - The Battle of Abiqua - was quickly squelched by the settlers. Twelve Indians, including Klamath Chief Red Blanket, and one white man, James Stanley, were killed. The battle was kept secret for nearly twenty years as Indian women, mistaken for warriors, were injured or killed by the whites and they were ashamed.

Crooked Finger derived his name from a deformed hand injured in an accidental discharge of a flint-lock rifle. His weakness was said to be the "blue ruin," a cheap rum from the Sandwich Islands. Crooked Finger was not found among the slain in the Battle of the Abiqua. According to Eldon Austin of Cedardale, legend has it, that Crooked Finger met his end after a bout with firewater. North of Mulino was a valley where the pioneers would camp when they traveled the two-day trip to Oregon City. Crooked Finger showed up one day, in an inebriated state, and the pioneers took the opportunity to get rid of him by clubbing him to death. His squaw carried him to his camp north of Mulino and buried him.

Another famous Molalla Indian was Indian Henry, for whom a Clackamas County park is named. He was the last chief of his tribe. He was a peace loving Indian who married a Klamath squaw and settled down on a farm on the north fork of the Molalla River. The principal band of the Molallas had ceded their lands on May 6, 1851, to the whites and were to receive $22,000 and a reservation. Most were sent to the 6,000 acre Grande Ronde Reservation at the headwaters of the Yamhill River. The younger Indians were more willing to go but the older men were reluctant as they wanted to pass their final days on familiar hunting grounds.

Indian Henry chose to live as a white man. His first squaw was an industrious, thrifty woman and excellent housekeeper. She earned a local reputation as a glove maker. When Henry killed a deer, she would tan the hide and make gloves and moccasins, providing the family a modest income. However, there were no children begotten in this relationship and Indian Henry blamed his wife for what was probably his fault.

Around 1880, Indian Henry fell in love with Beaver Trapper's daughter, and traded the old man some ponies for the young squaw. His first squaw was very upset when he brought the younger squaw home. She was disconsolate for weeks and one day she disappeared. After three days of searching they found her dead - dressed in fine clothes decorated with her own beaded work and a necklace of elk teeth. She had gone to the bank of Dickey Creek, fastened a rope to a limb of a tree and around her own neck and then jumped off the bank.

On September 13, 1913, with the coming of the first train to Molalla, Indian Henry dressed in all his finery and headed the parade. Appearing in feathers and the belt of authority of his father, he was a featured attraction at this historical event.

A few days later he was found dead. The September 25, 1913, issue of the Molalla Pioneer describes the circumstances:

"Tuesday morning, Dr. Todd was called by Judge Dungan to go to assist Henry Yelkes who was thought to be by the roadside near the Marsh farm in need of assistance. When the judge and Dr. Todd arrived they found the body of Indian Henry who had evidently been dead for some time as he was quite stiff. They at once sent to Oregon City and Coroner Wilson. Sheriff Mass came out in an auto.

"Harry Clark, who had been with Henry, had gone to town and called Dungan from Delta Austin's phone. The investigation showed that the ground had been tramped as if there had been a sort of a scuffle. The body had fallen with the head to the west and had been dragged by Harry to the side of the road about thirty feet distant. Clark was wearing a peculiar shaped shoe which fitted exactly into the tracks made by the person dragging the body. A bunch of hair was picked up in the road which had been pulled from Henry's head. The right side of his forehead was bruised and skinned by a blow of some hard substance. There was no money found on the body. Ten cents were found in the grass where it evidently fell when the pockets were being gone through.

"Clark asserted that his mind was blank from the time he left Mt. Angel with Henry until he awakened in the morning and not finding Henry called to him and when he received no answer he started down the road and found him lying by the road. To all questions his answer was "I don't remember." When Clark was searched a five dollar gold piece was found in the bottom of his shoe. Several silver dollars were found in a back pocket.

"At the inquest Dr. Todd testified that the wound in the head was not sufficient to cause death alone. The jury returned a verdict that Henry Yelkes had met death from unknown causes.

"A message was sent to Fred Yelkes (adopted son of Henry and his second wife), Henry's son, and he came home Wednesday morning. He was working in a logging camp near Winlock.

"He was buried Wednesday by the side of his first wife and father, at Dickey Prairie, the last home of the tribe.

"The passing of old conditions are emphasized by the sad death of Chief Henry, the last of the Molallas. His life was one which linked past savagery to present civilization. We suppose last Friday, riding at the head of the great procession and welcoming the first passenger train to the land formerly occupied by his father's people, was the proudest moment of his life. Judged from christian ethics his life has been far from perfect. The few who have known him from boyhood credit him with being honest, the white man's friend and trustworthy in every respect.

"The passing of a nation is a sad event. This tribe which, with Chief Henry's death passes completely out of existence once was powerful and, in their way, happy. The goodly place in which their lot was cast was, even by the Indian's standard, a prosperous one. The name Molalla, a corruption of the Indian word "Moo-la-la" means much grass, indicating fertility of the soil and foods for herds of game and later native horses. The white man "Came, he saw, he coveted," and with characteristic aggressiveness gradually crowded the tribe back to the hills and finally off of the earth. It is significant that the paleface's vice was directly instrumental in removing the harmless and peaceable sole representative of a once powerful tribe." -

The Molalla Indians.

* * *

PART TWO:

"War on the Abiqua"

by John Warnock

"Let me tell you something about these Klamath Indians, stranger. People tend to laugh a little at the Oregon Indians. Flat-heads, they calls them. But the Klamaths, let me tell you, were hanging on the tail of anybody - even the Cayuses who murdered the Whitmans.

"Now settle down, son, because this here story goes way back to the days when the Abiqua River valley was among the first settlements along the ridges of the Willamette. I settled there myself after I gave up on a stake I put out near where the Columbia and the Willamette came together - where the town of Portland is now.

"I got into this country by driving a herd of cattle up from California-most of the time along the Klamath trails. I knew them rattlesnakes. They were just kind of like coyotes - sneaking around until they saw an advantage.

"Anyway I finally put down my stake along the Abiqua. It was a real pretty little river - coming like it was out of the mountains and heading and tumbling over the rocks for about six miles. I got to know the Chinook language and because I dealt with them Klamaths who came up the trail near my place, both the Molallas and their cousins, the Klamaths and the Cayuses, came to hold pow-wows with me.

"Right after the Whitman squabble, people around the Abiqua got nervous - particularly when they heard a couple Cayuses were in the vicinity to try to get the Molallas and their visiting relatives, the Klamaths, to join in with them for a general uprising.

"Of course, now, you understand that many of the men around here who had struck out their own land claims, were so mad about the Whitman killing they volunteered right off to kill Cayuses. And that left a lot of women folks and little kids on the farms along the Abiqua to protect themselves.

"That friends, is where the Klamaths come in. Remember me telling you them Klamaths were kind of like rattlesnakes. They didn't get mean until they were awful sure they could get away with it. So the Molallas were acting as the rich cousins of that Klamath bunch and

between the two tribes they made themselves into considerable nuisances around here.

"They were breaking into many cabins stealing blankets. I was over at David Colver's helping him raise a barn along with the rest of the neighbors one morning when James Harpole's daughter, Betty, came rushing up and told us about how the Klamaths come into her house and took a sack of flour. Of course myself and everybody else at the barn-raising got horses and took off after them Klamaths. We didn't catch them, but we knew right then there was going to be trouble - and we were waiting for it.

"But you can see what was about to happen anyway. A bunch of us got together and began to organize volunteer units - because we knew there was going to be trouble. The bunch I was with was led by Richard Miller and we had good men from Butte Creek and some from Elliott's Prairie and all over this part of the valley.

"Now you remember I was telling you how it all started over two Cayuse scouts. Guess I better explain that to you a little bit. Them Cayuses were hard put to it and they were sending scouts all over Oregon to try to get neighboring tribes to get going with a coalition which would battle anybody who was white.

"It wasn't enough the folks around here were upset by the cattle which was disappearing, and the food that was being stolen by the Klamaths and the Molallas. When they were put to it to prove their innocence the Molallas just grinned at us and said they were innocent but made strong hints that their brothers, the Klamaths, were quite capable of stealing anything which wasn't tied down. The Klamaths weren't a bit afraid of doing the same thing and pointing out very vigorously that the Molallas had been known to snitch a little here and there.

"So you get the situation. The Indians got nothing but sassyiness, and we got nothing but sly looks.

"It was about this time of the year-early in March 1848. Two Cayuse scouts came to the village at which the Molallas and the Klamaths were bedded down. Word spread fast. Everybody around here knew them Cayuses were up to nothing good. They were trying to get the

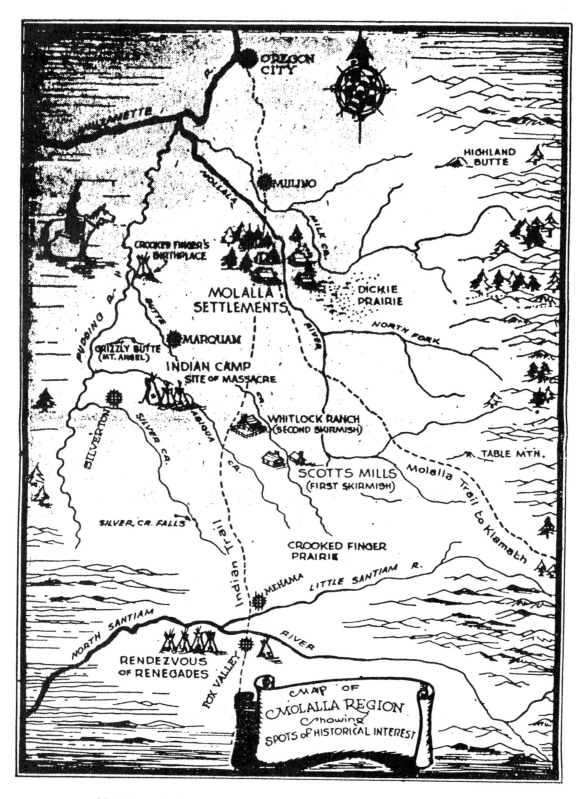

Map from the Oregonian, Sunday Magazine Section, April 29, 1934.
This map was probably drawn by or with the assistance of Dee Wright.

This rare photo shows a group of Molalla Indians at their camp above Dickey Prairie, east of Molalla. The photo was taken around 1870 by a Silverton photographer named Jones. *Photo courtesy of Pacific First Bank, Molalla.*

Molallas and the Klamaths to declare a general war and strike at the settlers who had stayed behind during the Cayuse War. That would put us in the same situation as some of the settlers in eastern Oregon when the Palouses and Nez Perces joined the Cayuses.

"We could see nothing else to do but get a party and have a talkfest with Coosta, the Molalla chief, who had something to say about how the Klamaths, the visiting tribe, acted up.

"We was just starting down the hill into the camp - that was on the place which was later settled by George Woolen - when we came upon the two Cayuses which were causing all the trouble. We did what anybody would have done, I guess. We took them prisoners and marched them back to a high place along the Abiqua and staked them out there with a couple of the boys to look out for them.

"The rest of us went back to the village and got a hold of Coosta. Thing that made us maddest at them Cayuses was their attitude. They just looked at us and hinted darkly that the Molallas were not going to kick the Klamaths out like we said we wanted them to do.

"Now this chief, Coosta, didn't receive us very cordially at all. We asked him as nice as we could about the Cayuses but he wouldn't give us any satisfaction at all. In fact he just told us in a sullen voice the Cayuses were guest of his and he would protect them. And that isn't the half of it. He pointed out the Klamaths were also his guests and they had the right to stay in the valley and they were also under his protection.

"Even though this was no real satisfaction, we might have gotten along alright with Coosta, but things began to happen. We heard shots coming from the ridge upstream where we had left the Cayuses with some of our boys guarding them. Just a few minutes later the guards came bounding down the hill. They told us the two Cayuses all of a sudden jumped off the 40-foot bank and into the Abiqua which was flowing swift and muddy from the spring snows melting. They said they shot at the swimming Cayuses but didn't even nick them.

"So we got out of the Molalla camp. We didn't know what was going to happen. But on the morning of March 4, a troop of about 50 Molallas and Klamaths came around to my cabin and in no uncertain terms asked me to go over to pow-wow. They were all dressed up in battle regalia and I didn't want to have much truck with them. But I didn't see much else to do.

"Anyway, I got my rifle and went out to meet them. I told Coosta I would come with him to Millers if he did it the way I wanted him to do it. He agreed. I put him in front of me, cocked my rifle, and he marched the rest of his men ahead. It took us maybe a half-hour-maybe forty-five minutes - to get over to Millers.

"All the way over Coosta turned to look at me. I kept my rifle cocked and Coosta I guess knew there would be one less Indian in his tribe if he tried anything.

"I didn't get the idea at first. But later I gathered that those durn fool Indians thought we had purposely killed the Cayuses who got away from our boys. And they wanted us to get together five horses for them as retribution.

"Of course, Dick Miller wouldn't listen to any of this. He just told them he wouldn't have anything to do with it, and furthermore said he knew the Cayuses weren't even dead.

"But figuring on getting along with them as good as possible, Miller offered the whole bunch-fifty, there was-dinner. Then Miller gave the signal and all the whites went into his cabin and closed the door. Outside, things got noisy. The Indians whooped it up a little and they even fired some shots into the walls of the cabin.

"Finally Coosta came up to the cabin, repeated the demands for the five horses. We were waiting for him. As soon as he got close, I grabbed him, yanked him inside and pulled a knife.

"I threw that Indian across a stool in the cabin and let him know that unless he cut out his foolishness there was going to be a bloody scalp hanging over Miller's door. Coosta showed the first intelligence he had shown all day.

"He ordered his warriors to get moving. I finally let him go, but not until he had threatened to cut my throat and that of both the Miller and the Patterson families.

"I guess all of this didn't go unnoticed up and down the valley. Because at that moment the word was traveling and the next morning the home guards started to show up at my cabin.

"We held a council of war, elected Daniel Waldo as our colonel, and decided the only way out of our troubles was to make sure them Klamaths left for home.

"So we set out toward Coosta's camp, but we split up into two companies. One - the one on the north side of the river - was led by Waldo and the other under Captain Geer went down the south side. The south side of the river was the woody side and I volunteered to act as a guide for the Geer company.

"Our original plan was for the companies on both sides of the river to hit Coosta's camp at the same time. We didn't want any bloodshed unless it was necessary, you understand. So everybody agreed there was no shooting to be done. We wanted just to get those Klamaths on the trail home.

"We started toward the Indian village. But we didn't get too far. The Molallas had scouts watching for us and Joe Churchill got excited when he saw one of the sentries break for the camp and he fired and the sentry fell.

"Then we all got off our horses and started toward the camp on foot. The Indians were all in a hustle. The Klamaths began to cross the river on a footlog. We just got out of the bushes when we were showered with arrows.

"That's when we started shooting. We had been in the woods all day in a drizzling kind of a rain and we found we couldn't fire half of the time because the old flintlocks we used in those days had become soaked.

"Come to think about it, those soaked rifles probably saved my life. Me and one of those Klamath warriors squared off. He had loaded first and pulled up, cocked and fired point-blank. I gave a little prayer and what do you think happened? Nothing.

"So I cocked my rifle, aimed carefully and figured I had a dead Klamath to my credit. But all I heard was a soggy click and the hammer snapped. Then it was the Indian's turn. Then mine. And finally Elias Cox came up from behind me, took aim, and fired, and the Indian dropped his rifle, jumped into the river and swam toward the other side.

"Now you understand this was all between us and the Klamaths. Coosta, the Molalla chief, and his men stayed out of it.

"The Klamaths looked like they were pretty much on the way by the time it got dark. Some of our boys came back up to my place and the rest of the men went back to their homes - because we half expected the hurt Klamaths to make raids on their unprotected cabins.

"During the night a light snow fell and in the morning we decided it was a good time as long as the Klamaths were on the run to keep them that way. We scouted up and down the stream and finally found some tracks. We followed these and after a while came on the Klamath camp.

"If them Indians figured on making a stand, they picked a good place. Their camp was set up in a little bog and it was almost surrounded with thickets of vine maple and underbrush.

"We advanced as close as we could. The Indians were waiting. As soon as we got close enough they let go with a shower of arrows. Then we opened fire and some of the warriors began to fall.

"Ten of them dropped and the Klamaths had enough. They started for the mountains. And they didn't come back.

"After that we went back to the Molalla village and laid down the law before them. We told what Klamaths were left, they would have three days to get on the trail for their home. We also gave Coosta a word of advice about living in these parts and the next morning we saw all the Klamaths head south. They never came back.

"The point of all this is just to show that those Klamath may not have been a real warring tribe. But if they were given a chance they could be mighty mean and sneaky.

"We were mighty near forced to get rid of them. And frankly I'm just as happy they never came back."

*   *   *

The Lament of the Umatilla

by Bert Huffman

Spirit of the Yesterday hovers near and croons —
Brings my heart the hunting grounds of the long-long Junes!
Sings of years forgotten, chants of races dead —
Weep, my wondering baby, for the Good Moons fled.

By the silvery river all your race has died —
Sleep and dream, my baby by its lisping tide!
Comes no more the hunter from the glorious chase —
O'er yon tempted mountains swarms the paler race.

Hark! I heard a whisper calling from the past —
Hear the warriors long-drawn cry on the tempest cast!
Hush, my heart, and listen! Calling, Calling, still —
Ah, 'tis but the moaning winter o'er the silent hill!

Hark, the hurried hoofbeats of the warrior band!
Ah, my heart betrays me in this empty land!
Sleep and dream my baby, by the teepee fire —
Nothing for thy kindling hope, nothing to desire.

Broken let thy young heart ache; crushed thy spirit brood!
What to thee the white man's ways worse than solitude —
By a dying watch fire crooning to the night —
Let the vanquished tribesmen pass from human sight.

* * *

CHAPTER III

The Vaughans of Molalla

"Vaughan First Pioneer to Hoist Wagon
Over Oregon City Bluffs" . . . . by Gail McCormick

The William Hatchette Vaughan house on South Macksburg Road in Molalla, Oregon, is an exquisite looking structure built in the Greek Revival-Italianate style. The house has an ornate single bay front porch with a balcony above surrounded by a cutout balustrade railing. A most unusual cobblestone foundation and front walk constructed of native rock still remain after 100 years of use. William Hatchette Vaughan was one of the original four donation land claimers that formed the four corners of Molalla. Today, ownership of the Vaughan house remains in the family. *Photo from the author's collection.*

Bibliography:
Hines, Rev. H. K. DD. "William Hatchette Vaughan," <u>An Illustrated History of the State of Oregon</u>, 1893
Nesmith, James W., "Diary of the Emigration of 1843," <u>Oregon Historical Quarterly #7</u>, December, 1906
Schulz, Blaine, "Pioneer Molalla Homestead Boasts Graceful Old Mansion," <u>Oregonian</u>, September 19, 1960
Vaughan, Champ Clark, "Uncle Billy of the Molalla Prairie," Published Manuscript, September, 1991

"Vaughan First Pioneer to Hoist Wagon Over Oregon City Bluffs"

by Gail McCormick

Twenty-two year old William Hatchette Vaughan arrived in Oregon City on the 1843 wagon train and started his search for the perfect spot to declare his donation land claim. He was looking for a piece of land well suited for farming and livestock grazing and generally flat and free of trees. His search ended sixteen miles south of Oregon City where he found a perfect tract of land on the Molalla prairie near the river. It was this prairie that the Molalla Indians periodically burned to perpetuate the growth of native grass to further their hunting and grazing purposes. Here William Vaughan staked out his donation land claim on a rectangular parcel of land. Later he was recognized as the first pioneer to bring a wagon into the Molalla area. Two other pioneers, William Russell and John Waggoner, had attempted to settle on the Molalla prairie but they abandoned their claims after a few weeks when they were driven away by the Indians. In 1845, with William's encouragement, they reestablished their claims. In 1848, Waggoner's claim was relinquished to Thomas P. Jackson.

William's first priority was construction of a log cabin, reinforced for protection from the Indians. Loneliness settled in early for this young bachelor with no sight of other white settlers for fifteen miles and about to encounter many small skirmishes with the Indians. He often had to laugh at himself when fear overtook him such as one evening when he ventured to a nearby spring for water. As he stooped down to bail some water he felt something brush his shoulder and he was certain that a Molalla Indian was about to "do him in." Trying to overcome his fear, he slowly turned and discovered only a low hanging limb of a tree on his shoulder!

But the Indians frequently gave him trouble that first year, and once he was attacked by a party of sixteen. With dauntless courage, he succeeded in making a miraculous escape. After this episode, and over a period of years, he established a trusting friendship with the Indians and they often depended upon him to mediate disagreements among tribal members. His expertise as a hunter, horseman, farmer and builder brought great respect from the Indians and neighboring settlers. He

William Hatchette Vaughan
"Uncle Billy"
1822 - 1906

soon became known as "Uncle Billy" to many.

Uncle Billy was a pioneer in the true sense of the word - "one who goes forward and removes obstacles for others." Traveling with the first wagon train to cut through to the Oregon Territory in 1843, he clung to his dream of building a large ranch in Oregon. He was descended from Scotch-Irish ancestors, who immigrated to the colony of Virginia early in the history of America, where they became people of wealth and influence. His father, James Vaughan, was born in Virginia, and there married Miss Nancy Hatchette. They settled in the Rutherford County of Tennessee and reared a family of thirteen children,

The William Hatchette Vaughan House built from 1882 - 1885. ca. 1903.

William being the fifth son. Later the family moved to Missouri.

William Hatchette Vaughan was born in Tennessee, January 17, 1822. At the age of sixteen, through an elder brother and the district congressman, arrangements were made for him to attend the military school at West Point. His father crushed this aspiration and he began an obsession to travel to the Oregon Territory. Rumors were flying about free land - up to 1,000 acres - in Oregon and for this young man the opportunity was too good to ignore. Leaving behind his parents, brothers and sisters, whom he would never see again, in May of 1843, he joined up with Peter G. Stewart's family wagon and the first great migration to Oregon. He alternated with Stewart's two sons driving ox teams over the 2,000 mile trail.

Early on William experienced a rude awakening of the dangers and challenges that lay ahead. Only four days out, the wagon train crossed the swift-running Kansas River, swelled with spring run-off. John Gantt had just joined the wagon train as the pilot, and a decision was made to attempt a river crossing at a location just west of the present city of Topeka, Kansas. As the river was too deep for fording, a crude raft was constructed to ferry the wagons and people across. The livestock had to swim across, and William volunteered to help keep the livestock moving in the cold river. During the crossing, he was immobilized by some painful cramps and began to struggle and disappear beneath the surface. James Nesmith rushed to his rescue and with the help of Peter Stewart, and after considerable effort, the two managed to get this now lifeless body to the shore. In an attempt to revive him, a wooden keg was brought to the traumatic scene by a young man named Edward Lenox and an early "cpr" rescue ensued. William was laid over the wooden keg and rolled back and forth to remove the water from his lungs while Stewart and Lenox pumped his arms. He revived and, refusing to be discouraged by a near

Reunion of the William Hatchette Vaughan family on March 3, 1903, on the occasion of the 70th birthday anniversary of Susan Mary Officer Vaughan. Photo includes all eleven of William and Susan's children. Front row from left: William Officer, William Hatchette, Susan Florida, Susan Mary, Cora Kuehn and John Calhoun. Back row from left: Mary Tennessee, Isom Crandall, Franklin White, Viola Evaline, Stonewall Jackson, Hardee Longstreet, and in the center, Nancy Virginia. In this photo, taken in front of the family home, the unique cobblestone foundation is visible in the lower right hand corner. *All Vaughan family photos are courtesy of Champ Clark Vaughan.*

catastrophe, after only a day's rest, he continued with his wagon train duties. On this wagon train there followed many notable events including a buffalo stampede; several encounters with Indians; a view of the Chimney Rock formation; and the passing visit of Lieutenant John Fremont with his party of U. S. Army Corps of Topographical Engineers who were conducting a survey expedition of the Oregon country.

The wagon train arrived at The Dalles in mid-October and the Stewart family party traveled down the Columbia River in canoes to Fort Vancouver. Friendly Indians brought them up the Willamette River to Oregon City.

Upon arrival in Oregon City, William went to work for the Hudson Bay Company as a fence and barn builder, thereby securing provisions and livestock before setting out to find his claim. He helped to clear brush, heavy fir trees and vine maple out of the area now known as Oregon City. Then there were just a few cabins near the falls. Abernethy had built a flouring mill and sawmill on the island, at the falls, called Mission Hill. William helped get out the timbers for Dr. McLoughlin's sawmill and helped build a log cabin where the courthouse now stands. He saw the water first turn on the wheel of the McLoughlin flouring mill.

August 27, 1847, William Vaughan and Susan Mary Officer were married in a double wedding ceremony shared with John K. Dickey and Martha Ann Officer. The Officer girls were from Tennessee. Their father, James

Officer, came to Oregon with his family of seven children in 1845 and settled on a donation claim, twelve miles south of Oregon City.

William and Susan Vaughan were industrious people and replaced the log cabin with a fine three-story home and other substantial buildings on their farm that comprised 960 acres at its peak. The house, begun by William in 1882, included two double fireplaces and was finished three years later. One of the choice remaining historic homes in the Molalla area, it is of Italianate style and has a most unusual cobblestone foundation and front sidewalk continuing across the front yard where a solid stoop was made to step into one's carriage or buggy. No money was put into building of the house. Lumber came from a sawmill erected on the farm and all other expenses for materials and labor were in trade or barter. This home on Macksburg Road in Molalla is still owned by the Vaughan family today.

William and Susan Vaughan had eleven children: Franklin White (b. 1849, m. Mary Ringo), Isom Crandall (b. 1852, m. Nancy Hungate), Nancy Virginia (b. 1854, m. Oren Cutting), Mary Tennessee (b. 1857, m. George T. Frazier), Viola Evaline (b. 1860, m. John Stubbs, later m. William H. Engle), Stonewall Jackson (b. 1862, m. Florence Patty), Hardee Longstreet (b. 1865, m. Neoda Mallatt), Susan Florida (b. 1868, m. Nathan Moody), John Calhoun (b. 1870, never married), Cora Kuehn (b. 1873, m. Jenks McCown) and William Officer (b. 1876, m. Eleanor Moody). William's southern heritage is clearly reflected in the given names of his children.

The family was of the Baptist faith. Politically William was a Democrat. Between 1868 and 1878, he was nominated three times for the Oregon State Legislature, but his party being in the minority, he was defeated. In the fall of 1847, after the murder of the Whitmans, along with his father-in-law he volunteered and served in the Cayuse war, furnishing his own horse and equipment. He was in the battle of Umatilla. The engagement lasted from nine o'clock in the morning until night, when the Indians withdrew.

"Uncle Billy" also became known as the "King of Hunters." A fine Kentucky rifle brought with him from his home in Tennessee served him well in Oregon. For many years he killed wolves and mountain lions that made havoc among his and the neighbors stock. It was a familiar sight to see him passing through town with his trained hounds, Ahi and Pomp, heading for the mountains to hunt for deer. His hounds and his guns were his delight and, even in his elder years, these choice hounds and the old rifle afforded him great pleasure.

William Vaughan passed away in 1906 and Susan Vaughan in 1911.

*   *   *

CHAPTER IV

The Wrights of Liberal

Although remodeled over the years, the Liberal Store today still projects the character of a by-gone era. *Photo from the author's collection.*

Bibliography:
Author Unknown, "Wright's Bridge Battered Landmark," *The Bulletin*, December 4, 1974
Crawford, Agnes, "W. J. Vick's Store Hub of Old Liberal," *The Bulletin*, November 13, 1974
Martell, Isabel, "Smallpox, Scourge of the Oregon Frontier," *Molalla Pioneer*, June 29, 1972
Nolan, Bertha of Milwaukie, Oregon, "Wright Family History," Unpublished Manuscript
Nolan, Bertha of Milwaukie, Unrecorded Interview, June, 1990

PART ONE:

"Area Congressman Struck Down by Smallpox"

by Gail McCormick

(The following is a fictional story based on fact and the Wright family stories handed down through the generations.)
Mary and Elizabeth, the family's younger children, were shouting "Daddy's home!" as Lizzie Wright hurried to the front door to welcome her husband, Congressman Harrison Wright. On this day in October, 1870, Lizzie was surprised to see her husband reel into the house, wide-eyed and his face flushed with fever. He had come home from the Oregon Legislature a very sick man.

Quickly, Lizzie escorted her husband to the bedroom, shooing away the younger children as she went. A woman very capable of taking command, she quickly assessed the situation and sent son Silas out to tend to Harrison's horse. Harrison was mumbling "Just a spell of

Harrison Wright (right)
1814 - 1870
and his brother, John Wright

grippe I guess," as she undressed him and gently put him to bed. Fear struck her heart as she realized this was unlike any grippe she had seen. He was chilled and Lizzie covered him with warm quilts. Baby Johnny crawled into the room to see what was going on and she picked him up and took him to the older girls to care for.

Frontier Wedding Bells Ring
As Lizzie nursed her husband of twenty three years, memories of their life together flooded her mind. She had

Elizabeth A. "Lizzie" Wright
1829 - 1921

*Mary Adaline
& Hester Ann Wright*

*Elgerine
& Oreantine Wright*

Elizabeth Wright

fallen in love the moment they met. How well she remembered their wedding day, February 25, 1847, when she had left the comfortable home of her mother and step-father in Waldo Hills and tied her total possessions in a square cloth and mounted the saddle in front of Harrison. Together they had ridden north to the little cabin on the beautiful Molalla River that was to be their home for many years. He was 33, she 18.

All eleven of their children had been born on this land that had come to be called Wright's Four Corners. She became saddened when she thought of their two beloved children, Sarah and Preston, who had died in infancy. Their deaths and the other struggles of frontier life had drawn Harrison and her so close together. They had been most fortunate with their other children, though. As in most large families, the older boys, Joseph, 22, Silas, 19, and Reuben, 13, helped with the family chores and the older girls, Oreantine, 17, and Elgerene, 15, helped with the younger children; Hester Ann, 10, Mary Adaline, 8, Elizabeth, 5, and baby Johnny, almost a year old now. How swiftly the years had gone by.

Harrison Wright
Becomes Congressman

Lizzie had been supportive of Harrison's desire to run for the Oregon Legislature, even though she knew it would mean sacrifices on her part as it meant he would be away from home often. Besides Harrison's congressional duties, they also had 640 acres to tend and he had been appointed postmaster and ran the local post office from their home. Harrison was a respected and public spirited man, a fine example for their sons, and he wanted to make this step into politics. Lizzie could pass out the mail and the boys could take care of the farm.

Lizzie sponged her husband's burning body. The fever seemed to be growing and Harrison was developing a blazing headache. Lizzie would not leave her husband's side for a minute. She thought of the time in 1849, when she and their first two babies had seen Harrison off to the gold rush in California. He had returned driving a herd of Spanish longhorns which had been the start of their cattle business. The herd had multiplied quickly on this fertile land that Harrison had chosen as his land donation claim. Their fortune had grown to include many horses and Harrison had cultured an interest in racing. Other gentlemen came often to enjoy this sport on the racetrack Harrison had built on the back acres along the road to Macksburg.

Covered Bridge Built

Lizzie thought of the dreams and plans Harrison and she had shared. There had been many. Just four years before, Harrison had petitioned to build a covered bridge over the Molalla River at the site where they operated a

Sam Oakley

Silas Wright
& Nate Trullinger

Joseph Austin Wright

All Wright family photos are from the collection of George Wright. ca. 1866.

ferry. The ferry had provided the first transportation over the river. Lizzie smiled to herself as she remembered the old cow bell that had hung on a tree on the other side. Neighbors would ring the bell and they would ferry over to get them. What a celebration they had when the covered bridge had opened. They had held a dance on the "approaches" or "aprons" as they were called. Silas had become a talented fiddler and his music had ensured that all had a great time. Later the county government had decided to buy all the covered bridges and make them a part of a public road system. Harrison and Gabe Trullinger, on the north side of the river, had each been paid $2,500 in gold for their interest in the bridge.

Lizzie Learns Grit

She had her moments, though, when she wished he were home more often. One such time was when the Indian Crooked Finger, fearing the whites would take over all the land, had stirred up other Indians to fight. Only a few followed him, as most of the Indians were friendly and, besides, they had been paid for the land. Those were fearful moments when she had to help load bullets for the guns so the men could fight off the Indians. Indians had come by her home but had been driven south. It saddened her as she remembered some Indians who had been so friendly they had taught her children to speak their language.

Lizzie had learned true grit when her family came over the Oregon Trail in 1843. That was before the Barlow Road was built and they had to raft down the mighty Columbia River. Once they were stranded for five days, ran out of food and became so hungry they boiled leather and ate it. They finally did make it to Oregon City. Harrison had fared better on his trip over the trail. He had come over in 1844 and, aside from one battle with the Indians, his trip had been calm.

Worst Fears Confirmed

Harrison seemed to have no interest in food, but Lizzie kept pouring weak tea into him, praying he would get well soon. A few days later, her worst fears were confirmed when a rash came out and she knew he had brought smallpox home from the Oregon Legislature.

Smallpox! The plague most-feared by everyone. Even the younger children had heard of it. But Lizzie didn't panic - her beloved husband and the children were her main concern. "Joe, Elgerene!" she called, "gather your ticks and bed covers and move everyone down to the cabin at the race track and don't come near the house for anything." She and baby Johnny had already been exposed, but perhaps the rest of the children would be spared. After awhile, baby Johnny became ill and his sisters returned him to her in the house.

Wright's Covered Bridge built by Harrison Wright in 1866 at Liberal near where the new bridge now stands. Before the covered bridge, people had to ferry across the Molalla River. *Photo courtesy of Mrs. Homer Stipp.*

Bad News Traveled Fast

The news had spread like wild fire that Harrison Wright had brought smallpox home from the legislature, even though the only communication was by word of mouth. Lizzie could hear the neighbors whip up their horses before they reached the front of her house and then go by in a dead run. Only one, Ephriam Ramsby, left groceries for them on the front stile from Pete Noyer's store in Molalla.

One dark night, she was startled to hear a knock on the door. "Who is it?" she called out. "Sam Oakley, Miz Wright," the voice answered. "I heard you had smallpox and I come to see if I could help out." She knew he was a bachelor who lived in Barlow, miles away. She hesitated and called out, "Are you sure you want to take the chance?"

"I'm Not Skeered"

"I had the smallpox in New York. I'm not skeered. Fust thing to do is get them vaccinated. I'll take keer of that. Just tell me is there a heifer up close?" Wondering what he would do, Lizzie told him where to find a heifer. (In well-settled areas in the east and in Europe, vaccination was being used, but it was not general on the frontier.) Sam Oakley went into Harrison Wright's bedroom and

picked several of the scabs from the pustules that covered him from head to foot and took them to the barn. He made some shallow scratches in the udder of the heifer and unto them rubbed the pus from the scabs.

Grieving Sons
Bury Father

By this time, Harrison's handsome face was horrible to see, it was so covered with pustules. The baby had come down with a high fever and the day the rash came out on his body was the day that Harrison was "gone." Lizzie had no time to grieve. Harrison would have to be buried immediately. With the help of Sam Oakley, Harrison and Lizzie's three sons Joe, Silas, and Reuben built a coffin. Time could not be taken for a proper funeral. A grave was dug extra deep and the burying took place in the dead of night. The three grieving sons loaded the rough casket on the back of the hack and drove one night to the Dibble Cemetery west of Molalla. They were a very small funeral party. (No stone ever marked this grave and it has been lost to generations in a pasture.)

Crude Vaccination
from Cowpox

Meanwhile, the heifer soon came down with cowpox. Sam Oakley was ready to proceed with his vaccinations.

Bravely, Lizzie submitted to it first. She was worried, but felt the children's only chance was this. The children all lined up to take their turns. Sam scratched their upper arms with a piece of broken glass and rubbed the pus from the heifers scabs into the scratches. (In those days, vaccination left enormous scars.)

Brothers Say Goodbye
to Baby Johnny

Two weeks after Harrison died, Johnny passed away. Joe and Reuben had the sad task of making the small casket and burying the baby beside his father. In spite of the vaccination, Silas and Elizabeth took the disease and Sam had moved them back to the house. Hester Ann came down with a light form (called varioloid) and escaped the deep pitting that scarred the bodies of her brother and sister for the rest of their lives. Silas came so near death that they had laid him out on the planks across the backs of two chairs in the parlor until his brother could make him a coffin. But the cool of the room had revived him from his coma and Lizzie had heard him groan and saw his eyelids flutter. She quickly hustled him back to bed and he pulled through.

Family Treasures
Destroyed
by Fumigation

When all the sick were on the mend, Lizzie submitted to the smallpox. She thought that the incubation period of two weeks had been prolonged, perhaps by the vaccination. She was to be left with the horrible scars the rest of her life, but she pulled through. After all the scabs and dead skin were shed, fumigation was the next step in ridding the house of this horrible pestilence. Lizzie watched, numb from the pain of the past weeks, as Sam and Joe took up her treasured, newly woven rag rugs, with their heavy padding of straw and carried them out to the bonfire that, hopefully, would rid them of this disease. All of the bedding was burned. Strong suds were used to wash walls and anything that would not burn was aired out.

Love Lasted
a Lifetime

Lizzie grieved often for her husband who had been cut down, at the age of fifty six, from what might have been a notable career. Although she lived to be 92, no other man crossed her path that could fire that spark in her heart that Harrison had.

*   *   *

A typical early 1900 hop yard crew - The Jordan Hopyard. *Courtesy of Molalla Historical Society.*

PART TWO:

Wright's Four Corners

by Bertha Wright Nolan

After Harrison Wright's death, his land was divided between his eight remaining children. Reuben Wright, born 1857, inherited his share of the land donation claim and planted a hop yard where Arrowhead Golf Course now stands. He was a successful farmer and traveled extensively to Hawaii, New York and Kansas. On one trip back east he met Miss Addie Willet, a school teacher who wrote a regular column in a Kansas paper. He had read the column and had been corresponding with Addie before his trip east.

Reuben and Addie Marry

Reuben and Addie became man and wife June 16, 1892,

in Logan County, Oklahoma. The adoptive parents of Addie Willet, Frank and Louisa Catherine Willet, objected to this marriage but soon followed the couple back to Oregon. Granny Willet became the postmistress at Wright's Four Corners and ran the small store. She is credited with renaming the store area Liberal after Liberal, Kansas. Reuben and Addie worked the hop ranch. While in Oregon they had three children: Frank W. Wright (b. 1893), Harrison Wright (b. 1895), and Reuben Wright Jr. (b. 1897).

Cherokee Strip Calls

When the news that the Cherokee Strip of Oklahoma

The Reuben Wright Family: Front row from left: Alfred and Katherine. Middle row from left: Addie and Reuben. Back row from left: Reuben, Jr., Frank and Harry. ca. 1903. George and Agnes were born after this picture was taken. *Photo courtesy of Bertha Wright Nolan.*

The Hop Factory at Liberal that Reuben Wright operated stood where Arrowhead Golf Course now stands. Standing on the ramp from left: Silas Wright, Bob Coates and Reuben Wright, Sr. ca. 1897. *Photo courtesy of Agnes Wright Crawford.*

was to be opened for homesteading, Reuben sold his land and packed up his family, including in-laws, and headed for Oklahoma. Frank Willet and Reuben Wright each claimed 160 acres near Enid, Oklahoma. In Oklahoma, five more children were born: Katherine H. (b. 1899), Alfred T. (b. 1902), George O. (b. 1908), Inez E. (b. 1910). and Agnes J. (b. 1914). For many years the family suffered through Oklahoma storms, droughts and cyclones. In 1916, after eighteen years, Reuben sold the buildings, leased the land for pasture and came back home to Oregon, only hoping someday oil would be discovered. It did not happen in his life time.

Garden of Eden Developed
Back in Oregon, Reuben purchased fifteen acres of the original land claim from his sister Elizabeth Coates. This

land was on the east side of Highway 213 and this property is still in the family today. Reuben made a "garden of Eden" out of this acreage. He had a large fruit orchard with every kind of apple, pear, cherry, peach and peach-plum trees. He even had crab apple and quince. He planted strawberries, raspberries, gooseberries, currents, white grapes and blue grapes. He raised his own vegetables and feed for the cows, pigs and chickens. He had his own wheat ground at Union Mills. After living in the hot sandy state of Oklahoma and not being sure of growing anything, it was truly wonderful to be back home in the beautiful green state of Oregon. Reuben also worked as a carpenter to supplement farm income.

Reuben died in 1942 and Addie died in 1946. They are buried at Adams Cemetery.

* * *

Approximately 1911, the present Liberal Store building was built by W. J. E. Vick and later a home, thought to be a Sears and Roebuck precut home, was built to the right of the store. Both still stand today. Mr. & Mrs. Vick and their only child, Frances, lived there. The large area over the store was originally a dance hall and meeting place. Agnes Crawford describes Liberal in the 1920s as "a thriving community when Southern Pacific Railway made two round trips a day between Canby and Molalla. The Willamette Valley Southern Trolley was making four round trips daily from Oregon City to Molalla. There was a board sidewalk from the store up to the church on the hill. It was great fun to walk up the board sidewalk to the Southern Pacific Station, catch the train to the Canby Fair, stay all day and come back that evening. The passenger coach had elegant red plush seats. Also, one could catch the WVS at North Liberal Station, ride to Molalla, do your shopping and always be sure to stop at 'Doc Sailers' Ice Cream Parlour for a treat." The Buick touring car in front of the store is occupied by Otto Friedrich, behind the wheel, and his father, Bernhard Friedrich, seated in back. Others in picture unknown. *Photo courtesy of Richard Holmes, present owner of the Liberal Store.*

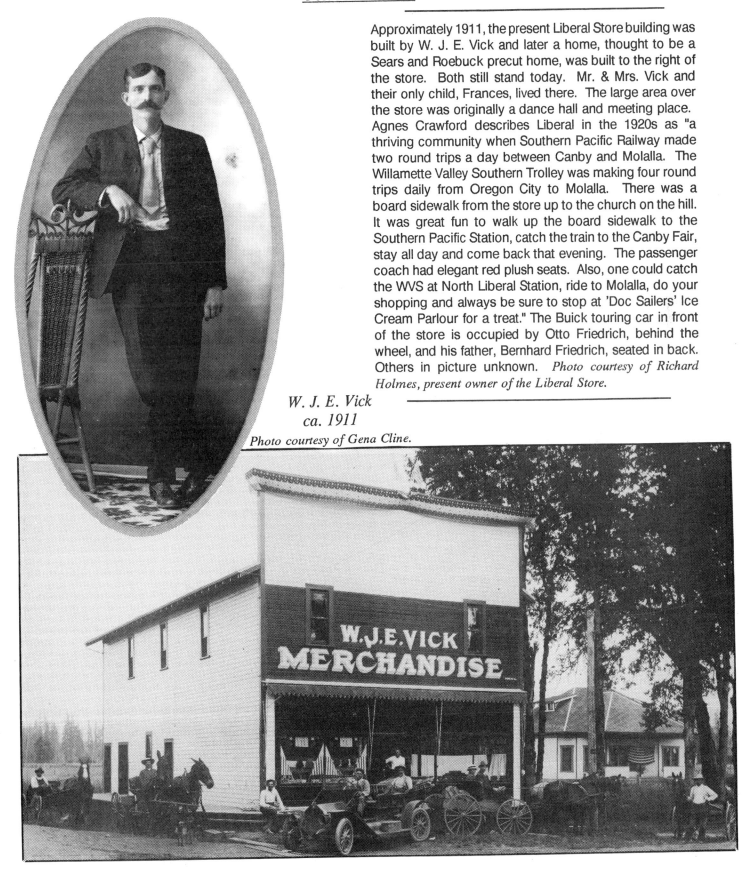

*W. J. E. Vick
ca. 1911*
Photo courtesy of Gena Cline.

The original Liberal Store was located across the street from the present store and was owned by Fred Burns, who is leaning against the corner post in this picture. In back of the store is a livery stable. A Mr. GPA Morey, in the long coat, is the only other person identified. *Photo courtesy of Richard Holmes, present owner of the Liberal Store.*

CHAPTER V

The Engles of Molalla

"Engles Hold Claim to Proud Heritage" . . . . by Gail McCormick

Four generations of Molalla's early families are represented in this 1906 photograph.
Back row: in the middle Clay and Victoria Vaughan Engle with their first son, Samuel Engle. They are flanked by Clay's mother, Nancy Noyer Engle, on the left and Victoria's mother, Nancy Hungate Vaughan, on the right.
Front row from left: Delilah Noyer (Clay's maternal grandmother), Nancy Duniway Engle (Clay's paternal grandmother), Susan Mary Officer Vaughan (Victoria's paternal grandmother) and Grandmother Hungate (Victoria's maternal grandmother).

Photo courtesy of Blanche Engle.

Bibliography:
Engle, Blanche, of Mulino, Oregon, Recorded Interview, April, 1990
Engle, Ed of Molalla, Oregon, Recorded Interview, June, 1990
Hines, Rev. H. K. DD. "Samuel Engle," An Illustrated History of the State of Oregon", 1893
"William Engle," The History of the Melchor Engle Family", 1937

"Engles Hold Claim to Proud Heritage"

by Gail McCormick

Samuel Engle, another of the honored Oregon pioneers of 1845, was born in St. Clair County, Illinois, January 30, 1831. His ancestors came from Germany and were among the early settlers of Virginia. Great-grandfather John Engle and his son Joseph fought in the Revolutionary War. The latter was the father of three sons and one daughter.

The eldest of these sons, William Engle, father of Samuel, was born at Harper's Ferry, Virginia, March 18, 1789, and was a soldier in the War of 1812. He was married in Virginia, in 1816, to Miss Mary Butt, and in 1820 they moved to Illinois, where she died in 1823, leaving

The Samuel Engle Family: Front row from left: Clarence Engle, Samuel Engle, Nancy Duniway Engle and Albert Engle. Back row from left: Annie Engle Everhart, Dee Engle, Alice Engle Harless, William Harold Engle and Emma Engle McFadden. *ca. 1895.*   *Photo courtesy of the late Ed Engle.*

William Everhart and his wife Annie Engle Everhart
Photo courtesy of Blanche Engle.

---

three children. In 1824, William married Mrs. Ester Hayes, who died soon after her marriage, and in 1826 he wedded Mrs. Martha Chance, who was born in 1798. She was a daughter of the famous William Clark of Lewis and Clark. They had five children, and with his wife and these children - then all single - he crossed the plains to Oregon in 1845. Samuel was then fourteen years old.

Family Departs for Oregon

The Engle family left their home in Illinois on March 18, 1845, their outfit consisting of two wagons, eight yoke of oxen, thirty-one cows and heifers, and three horses, the family being loaded in one wagon and their provisions in the other.

On this first trip across the plains, William Engle was captain of the emigrant train. The family had a successful journey and arrived in Oregon City in December of that year. They spent the winter there, where the father worked at the carpenter's trade.

In the spring of 1846, they selected a donation land claim in Clackamas County, sixteen miles south of Oregon City on the southeast corner of what was later to be called the Four Corners of Molalla. They built a hewed-log house. At that time there was only one settler between them and Oregon City.

In 1866, the farm on the Four Corners was sold to Oliver Robbins. William Engle then purchased a half section of land in Yamhill County, and after living on it a year, sold

out and went to Silverton in Marion County. There he purchased a tract of land and spent the remainder of his life. He died May 18, 1868.

William was influential in the early history of the Oregon Territory and state, serving in the Territorial Legislature in 1847 and was judge of Marion County for two years. He was an exemplary member of the Baptist Church for 45 years. His name ranks with the early pioneers who followed the example set by Dr. Marcus Whitman and thereby saved the Oregon Territory from going to Great Britain and becoming a part of Canada. His great intelligence and judgment were well-proven by the fact of his early ascendancy to influence and recognition after his arrival in the territory.

Samuel Engle subsequently purchased 235 acres of his father's original land claim on the Molalla prairie and resided there. In 1849, when only eighteen years of age, he sought the gold mines of California. He spent about six months mining on Clear Creek and also mined in Jackson, Oregon. In the early 1860s he ran a pack train between The Dalles and Canyon City and later ran an eight horse wagon on the same route.

Samuel Marries Nancy Duniway

Samuel and Miss Nancy H. Duniway married on November 16, 1854. A native of Illinois, she was born February 16, 1838, to Benjamin I. Duniway. Later her brother, Benjamin, married Abigail Scott. Abigail, with

Benjamin's help, fought for equal rights for women for 40 years. She won women the right to vote and became known as the "mother of Oregon equal suffrage."

Samuel and Nancy settled on the farm on the Molalla prairie. In 1875 they built a comfortable and substantial home there. This property he developed into one of the finest farms in the county.

Samuel Engle was thoroughly posted on the history of our state. An active and intelligent member of the Democratic party, he was several times chosen for positions of importance. The Democrats, however, being in the minority in Oregon then, he was always defeated. He took an active interest in the educational affairs of his district and served as school clerk for twenty years. He

Clyde Engle and his wife Zella Adams Engle
Photo courtesy of Blanche Engle

Hattie Miller Engle's Family
Mabel Miller Lay, Thomas Miller, Arch Miller, Hattie
Pierce Miller, Eliza Cook Miller
All photos this page are courtesy of Blanche Engle

Hattie Miller Engle & Hubert Engle

was a charter member and served as secretary of the grange.

The Engle Children

Samuel and Nancy had seven children, namely: Clarence, Emma F., Albert, William Harold (Harl), Alice, Dee and Annie. Clarence (1855-1904) married Miranda Long and had six children: Hubert, William, Clyde, Otis, Viola and Leona. Emma (1858-1923) married Thomas McFadden. Albert (1861-1924) married Nancy Noyer Ringo and had sons, Albert Clay and Samuel W. William (1863-1922) married Sara Harless who died. He then married Viola Vaughan. His children were Bernice, Inas and Gilbert. Alice (1870-1947) married Benjamin Franklin Harless and had children Vesta, Ruth, Perle Samuel, Berneita and Clarence. Dee (1872-1947) married Effie Adams and had sons Ross, Kenneth, Marlin and Elmer. Annie (1875-1961) married William Everhart and had one child, Reva May.

Samuel died in 1902 and Nancy in 1915. Many Engle descendants still reside in the Molalla area.

* * *

CHAPTER VI

The Klingers of Macksburg

"Klinger Descendant Still Resides on Original
Donation Land Claim" . . . . .by Gail McCormick

Dee Wright and Francis Klinger on the Klinger's donation land claim west of Liberal, Oregon, near Macksburg. ca. 1870. The original donation land claim was filed by Francis' father, John Klingler. Wright, a descendant of Harrison Wright, lived with Klinger before Klinger's marriage to Cora Comer. Dee Wright furnished much of the historical information available on the Molalla Indians. *Photo courtesy of Dorothy Felix.*

Bibliography:
Bird, Marie Klinger of Macksburg, Oregon, Recorded Interview, November, 1990
"Louis J. Klinger", Illustrated History of Central Oregon, 1905
Steininger, Lydia Klinger, "Klinger Family, German Immigrants", The Bulletin,
Steininger, Lydia Klinger, "Klinger Family History", Unpublished Manuscript

"Klinger Descendant Still Resides on Original Donation Land Claim"

by Gail McCormick

Written December, 1990
Marie Klinger Bird passed away December 4, 1991.

Early one morning I received a phone call from an elderly lady. Little did I know I was about to meet the oldest living descendant of the Klinger family - Marie Klinger Bird, age 94. She leaves a lasting impression on one. A small boned, feisty lady, when interviewed, Marie would periodically jump up to "get more wood for the stove". Today she resides with her daughter, Phyllis Syron, on two acres of the original donation land claim of her grandfather, John L. Klingler, whose last name was derived from the German version of the name Klingler. Marie was born in her father's log cabin not far from her present home on Macksburg Road about two miles west of Liberal, Oregon.

Marie stated that "in my life I did lots of things - everything a man could do. For years I plowed with a walking plow, sowed grain, cut wheat, cut and baled hay and milked cows. I raised around 300-350 chickens each year."

She remembers her childhood years when Indian Henry would come to visit and sometimes stay for a week. Indian Henry had been her father's playmate as a child. He often visited the Klinger home, and Marie and her family knew him well.

Born March 8, 1896, Marie married John Anderson in 1918. They divorced and she later married Burt Bird. Phyllis is an only child, but the extended Klinger family is large. Marie's father, Francis, was one of 15 surviving children of his generation. Many Klingers married into other founding families in the Molalla area including the Callahans and Ramsbys.

Family Arrived in Oregon in 1847

Marie's grandfather, John L. Klingler, was born in 1810 at River Rhine, Germany. He and the first Mrs. Klingler, Marie Therese Westhof, were married in Germany. They immigrated to the United States, sometime between 1834 and 1836 and settled in Warren County, Missouri. Marie

Cora and Francis Klinger with their two oldest children, Ona and Marie. ca. 1896. *Photo courtesy of the late Marie Klinger Bird.*

Therese Klingler died in 1844 and John Klingler then wedded Maria Anna in December, 1844, and together they made the overland journey to Oregon.

In 1847, the Klingler family was among the first to cross the Cascades with ox teams on the Barlow road, which was completed that year. Towards the last of the trip, a scanty supply of rice with a small allowance of bread made up their sole provisions. Their journey to Oregon was fraught with hardships and peril. At that time there were seven children and along the way another child, William Thomas, was born.

When the family finally came upon The Dalles, Lewis Klinger, then ten years old, spying the only house in The Dalles shouted, "A house, a house!". This was the first building they had seen since leaving Independence, Missouri, with the exception of Forts Laramie, Hall and Boise. They had seen many campers along the road who had killed their last ox for food. It is estimated that seven thousand immigrants started for Oregon that year, hundreds who died en route and were buried between the wagon tracks on the trail to Oregon. This was done to keep the Indians, which roamed the plains, from digging up the bodies and stealing the clothing in which the dead were buried. Hundreds more reached Oregon in a starving condition.

When the Klingler family arrived in Oregon City, the father had only twenty-five cents in money, and wheat was worth six dollars a bushel. Dr. McLoughlin, for many years with the Hudson Bay Company, sold John grain, taking his note for promise of payment. The family settled for two years on a land claim at Maple Lane near Oregon City. That claim was later reclaimed by a Mr. O'Connor, so the Klingler claim was moved to an area between Liberal and Macksburg in 1849.

At Macksburg, John and Maria quickly built three one-room log cabins to house their family. A larger, more spacious family home was completed in 1851. Marie Bird's father, Francis, learned to crawl in the new family home. (About 1969, this home was sold to Eric Ladd who in turn dismantled it and numbered each piece. He then packaged it, including window and door frames and the bricks from two huge fireplaces and hauled them to the coast where he rebuilt the home for himself. A lot of beautiful hand hewn lumber went into the building of this home.)

In 1859, tragedy struck the Klinger family, which had grown to 13 children. John L. Klingler and a neighbor were returning from Oregon City and while crossing the Molalla River in high water, he was thrown from the wagon. He suffered a massive skull fracture. Marie remembers her father, Francis, telling her that after his father was injured he never left his side until he died one week later, on November 28, 1859. John L. Klingler is buried in the small Klinger Memorial Cemetery on Klinger Road. That year, 1859, an infant son was also born and died. After John Klingler's death, the donation land claim was divided amongst his heirs: Maria Anna, Christina Willemine, 24, Matilda, 22, Lewis Johannes, 21, Therese Maria, 20, Helena Mariah, 18, Gustavus Ernst, 16, William Thomas, 12, Frederick Augustus, 10, Francis Clifton, 8, Elizabeth, 6, Emelia, 4, and Josephine, age 2.

Maria Anna Klinger, the mother, then wedded John Smith in 1864. They had two children: Lily Rosina, who died at age 3 and Ida Florinda. (Ida married John

John L. Klingler
1810-1859

Marie Klinger Bird
1896-1991
Marie Klinger Bird resided on the original donation land claim of her grandfather, John L. Klingler, until her death Dec. 4, 1991.

Maria Anna Klingler
1825 - 1890

The Francis Klinger family in front of the home still standing on Macksburg Road. ca. 1905. Left to right: Frederick, Lydia, Hazel, Marie, Orville, baby Willard, mother Cora Comer Klinger and Francis Klinger. On horse is Ona Klinger, Dorothy Felix's father. *Photo courtesy of Dorothy Felix.*

Reasoner Cole in 1867.) Maria Anna died January 24, 1890, and John Smith died July 5, 1880.

Francis Clifton Klinger (b. 1851)

When he grew up, Francis Clifton Klinger built a pioneer home on his share of the property along with many outbuildings. (This home on Macksburg Road still stands but has been extensively remodeled.) He waited to marry until age 42. He was a farmer, as most of the Klinger family had been, and also helped and took care of young boys who had left home. He taught them to become better young men as they grew into manhood. One of these young men was Dee Wright. Francis was said to be a man of fine character and was a helpful neighbor. He was very well thought of by people in the area.

Francis married Cora Belle Comer, daughter of William Henry and Mary Ellen Lee Comer of the Colton area in 1893. Together they had nine children: Ona (b. 1893, m. Myna Bonney, later m. Vera Oesser), another infant baby who died at birth, Marie Anna (b. 1896, m. John Anderson, later m. Burt Bird), Lydia May (b. 1898, m. John Henry

Steininger), Frederick (b. 1905, never married), Hazel Enid (b. 1902, m. Byron Harkness, later m. Charles Cross), Melissa Lorena (b. 1908, m. Lee Lester Williams), Willard Lewis (b. 1906, m. Irma Rose Connett), and Orville (b. 1900, m. Rose Gerbert, later m. Frances Adams Westberg). Marie Bird, age 95, and Melissa Williams, age 82, of Oregon City, outlived all their brothers and sisters. Francis and Cora Belle are buried in the Adams Cemetery near Molalla.

Lewis Johannes Klinger (b. 1837)

Lewis Klinger grew to manhood in Macksburg and in 1863 went to Wasco County and settled on Eightmile Creek, four miles northeast of Dufur, where he engaged in farming and stock raising. He married Melissa J. Woodcock, who was born on the plains in 1844 while her parents, Wilson D. and Keziah (Bunton) Woodcock, were en route to Oregon. (The Woodcocks settled on the Molalla prairie in 1861.) Lewis and Melissa did not have any children but raised a number of orphans.

In one five mile trip, while teaming in the Wasco County,

Lewis crossed the Eightmile Creek one hundred and nineteen times en route to Boise, Idaho. He made a success of farming and stock raising by buying calves cheap in the Willamette Valley and taking them to the rich grass pastures of Wasco county. He sold the products of his farm and cut the wild grass and hauled it to The Dalles where it readily sold for $20 a ton. In these various ways, Lewis accumulated and invested his first $1,000.

Lewis was a pioneer in more ways than one. He, in partnership with John McHaley and John Doyle, bought the first thresher used in Wasco County. It was called a Sweepstakes and swept the chaff from the wheat. He had taken out patents on several inventions, one of them a weeding machine, being of inestimable value. He also invented a baling press and hand hay press, which were not patented.

In 1889, he had amassed a modest fortune and selling his farm, he moved to the town of Dufur. He was an enthusiastic hunter, and fisherman, passing a large portion of the summer in the mountains. He was recognized as a progressive, broad-minded and influential citizen and served two terms as mayor of Dufur, but cared more for his superior camping outfit than for political honors.

The Other Children
of John L. Klingler

Christina Willemine, born 1834 in Germany, married Clifton Rhodes Callahan in 1851. He received part of his father's donation land claim. They had 13 children: John (b. 1852), David (b. 1853), George (b. 1855), Mary Jane (b. 1857), Louis (b. 1860), Martha (b. 1862), Dale Jon (b. 1864), Vienna (b. 1873), twins Rosena and Rosanna (b. 1875), and Ella Jane (b. 1880). Clifton and Christina Callahan are buried in the Callahan Cemetery on the original Callahan donation land claim near Dickey Prairie.

Matilda, born in 1836, married Woody Paujade who passed away. They had two children: Isodora and Frank William. Matilda later married Bill Gribble and moved to Gold Hill, Oregon. When he passed away she married Henry Klock.

Therese Maria, born in 1839, married a Mr. King, who passed away. They had two children: Elsie and Clara. Later Therese married Joseph Hiram Martin.

Helena Mariah, born in 1841, married David C. Morris. Their children were Mary Louisa (b. 1861, m. Edwin Albert Howard), John (b. 1863), Juliet Francis (b. 1864), Edwin (b. 1866), Ira (b. 1868), Otis (b. 1872), Frank (b. 1874), Charles (b. 1878) and Rose Anna (b. 1885).

No other information was found about Gustavus Ernst, born in 1843, Maria, born in 1846 and Frederick born in 1849. William Thomas was born in 1847 and died in 1866.

Elizabeth Marie, born in 1853 married George Wyland in 1858 and resided in the Molalla area.

Emilia, born in 1855, married Horace Siever Ramsby, in 1880, one of Molalla valley's best known farmers and pioneers. Horace Ramsby had the unique experience of spending his entire life on one farm, where his father Maxwell Ramsby had filed the original donation land claim. Their children were: Delbert, Carl, Alta (m. Glen Centril), and Rhoada (m. Herschel Wilson).

Josephine, born in 1857, married James W. Smith in 1885. She spent her entire life in the county. Their children were Chester, Ida (Howell) and Lela (Brown).

*   *   *

CHAPTER VII

The Trullingers of Union Mills, Oswego & Astoria

"Gold Rush Foretold on Oregon Trail" . . . . by Gail McCormick

One steps back in time when visiting Union Mills today. Still owned and operated by members of the Trullinger family, the two remaining buildings are well kept. The gracious white house, built in 1908 by Dellazon Trullinger, oversees and compliments the Union Mills farm supply building.

Bibliography:
Author Unknown, "Friedrich-Trullinger Nuptials," <u>Molalla Pioneer</u>. June 18, 1914
Author Unknown, "John Corse Trullinger," <u>Oregon Native Son</u>
Author Unknown, "Mills Center of Milk Creek Community," <u>The Bulletin</u>, April 9, 1975
Friedrich, Alvin of Canby, Oregon, Recorded Interview, March, 1990
Friedrich, Alvin, "Trullinger Family History," Published Manuscript
Furey, John, "Oswego Roots," <u>The Oregonian</u>, January 25, 1990
Gaston, Joseph, "Daniel Perry Trullinger," <u>The Centennial History of Oregon</u>, 1912
Goodall, Mary, "A New Era of Big Dreams," <u>Oregon's Iron Dream</u>", 1958
Hines, Rev. H. K. "Gabriel Johnson Trullinger," <u>An Illustrated History of the State of Oregon</u>, 1893
McArthur, Lewis L. "Union Mills," <u>Oregon Geographic Names</u>, 1974
Oliphant, Mary, "The Tale of Two Families," Published Manuscript, 1984
Trullinger, Gabriel, "Crossed Plains in 1848," <u>Oregon City Enterprise</u>, April 21, 1906
Trullinger, John Corse, Letter to the Editor, <u>The Oregonian</u>, Januay 12, 1890
Trullinger, John. C., "How Discovery of Gold in California Was Miraculously Announced," <u>Oregonian</u>, January 12, 1890

"Gold Rush Foretold on Oregon Trail"

by Gail McCormick

In 1848, the Trullinger family of thirteen traveled 2,000 miles on a journey that took six months to reach the Oregon Territory. Along the way, the discovery of gold in California was miraculously announced. John Corse Trullinger, then 20, related the story in a letter to the editor of the Oregonian in 1890:

"I crossed the plains from Iowa to Oregon in the summer of 1848 with my father's family. The company that we traveled with from St. Joseph, on the Missouri River, to Fort Hall was called Wambo's company. Captain Wambo had been in Oregon and California some years before and was a very competent man to take charge of an emigrant train. Nothing of importance transpired with us from the Missouri River to Fort Hall, with the exception of meeting Joe Meek on his mission to Washington, and the old mountain men, Eberts and Lebo.

"What we saw at the time, and with me ever since, has been a great phenomenon I shall now describe. We were camped on Sweetwater River about twenty miles east of Independence Rock; our corral made, teams out to grass, supper over and all gathered in little groups about the corral talking the things of the day that had just passed. As usual on such occasions upon a beautiful sunset in that lovely country of blue skies in the month of June, everyone was enjoying the beautiful weather and balmy evening. This was the 20th of June, 1848.

"It was perhaps thirty minutes after sunset when at the horizon in the southwest there began to rise up as it were a gold bronze ball. It looked about the size of a full moon. It very gently arose until it stood at what you would call the eight o'clock mark in the afternoon. There it stood still for a few minutes, then commenced to elongate each way across the horizon until it was in appearance about an inch wide. Then it commenced to crook up, and when it stopped its movement it made the word "mines". There it stood in the heavens in living letters of gold, and remained so until the darkness of the night faded it out. It stood there over three hours as plain as any sign over any store in the city of Portland, and as easily read.

Gabriel Johnson Trullinger
1824-1906
Founder of Union Mills

"The comments at the time by our old fathers and ministers were varied. Some divided the word - said it read mi-nes - that is , we would all get out to Oregon "mines" meaning flat broke. At that time no one on the plains knew of the discovery of gold in California. There was various comment on this phenomenon for some weeks, but no one could make it out.

"Finally, when we reached Oregon City, we heard of the gold mines in California, and that solved the problem. From that day to this, I have never doubted the story of the sword that hung over Jerusalem for seven years, and that there was a great and living God that on the eve of great events does communicate with men."

Hunting and Fishing
Good in Oregon

The decision to undertake the long journey to Oregon was made by Elizabeth Amanda Trullinger, mother of ten children. Her three oldest sons, Gabriel, 24 (b. 1824, m. Sarah Glover), Nathan H., 22 (b. 1826, m. Frances Greshen), and John Corse, 20 (b. 1828, m. Hannah Boyle), had heard that hunting and fishing were good in the Oregon Territory and were ready to leave when Elizabeth decided it would be best if the whole family went together. The other children were Amanda, 18 (b. 1830, m. John Wright then Mr. Hodson), Mary Jane, 15 (b. 1833, m. Andrew Cutting then A. B. Falkner), Elizabeth Ellen, 12 (b. 1836, m. Harbison Morgan), twins Eliza (b. 1838, m. Rene Matson or Mattoon) and Evangaline, 10 (b. 1838, m. William Lowe), Daniel Perry, 8 (b. 1840, m. Emily Wood), and little Sara, 5 years old (b. 1843, m. Mr. Todd). Along with Nathan's wife, Frances, and father, Daniel, they set out for Oregon on April 6, 1848, with three wagons. One was drawn by four yoke of oxen. Their entourage included cows, chickens, pigs and several horses. A family had to be quite well-to-do to travel the Oregon Trail as they had to be outfitted in advance for six months of travel.

Mother Was Future
President's Niece

Elizabeth Amanda Johnson and Daniel Trullinger married on April 27, 1823. She was the daughter of Archibald Johnson, brother of Andrew Johnson, Vice President under President Lincoln. He later became President when Lincoln was assassinated.

Elizabeth was described as a very wise and determined woman who looked after the health and education of her children. She was also a poet, song writer and herb doctor. Her strong character was an inspiration for her children and grandchildren. Daniel Trullinger, at the age of 22, was a part-time minister for the Christian Church. He was also a farmer in Indiana.

Union Mills Flour Mill built in 1877 by Gabriel Trullinger, has remained in the same family since founded. The sawmill pictured on the next page was built in 1854. Photo ca. 1908. *All Union Mill photos are courtesy of Alvin Friedrich.*

Oregon - Finally!

The family arrived in Oregon and took the Barlow Trail from The Dalles. When they arrived at the toll gate, near what is now Rhododendron, they had to pay by promise as they did not have enough money left to pay the toll. They arrived in Oregon City on September 14, 1848, and wintered there.

The first year in Oregon, Gabriel worked in Oregon City at his native trade of cabinet-making. Nathan and Frances headed ten miles south of Oregon City and settled on Milk Creek near what is now Union Mills. They built a cabin and started to cultivate the land. A donation land claim was filed for this land in the Trullinger name.

California or Bust!

In 1849, the excitement of the Gold Rush broke. Father Daniel with sons, Gabriel and John Corse, traveled by horseback to California. Daniel, being forty seven years old, soon found panning gold too hard a work for his age, gave up and returned home.

Gabriel and John stayed for two years and returned home with a small fortune, having sometimes panned $80 per day in gold. John is said to have brought back $18,000.

The United States was offering free land for the claiming in Oregon - 320 acres for single people and 640 acres if you were married. Apprehensive that gold might become overly plentiful and land therefore would become more

Gabriel Trullinger in 1898, at age 74, with grandchildren Pauline and Grant Trullinger, 8 and 11 years. (Children of Dellazon and Maude.) At the age of 14, Grant drowned in the Old Lake, leaving three sisters; Pauline, Maude and Blanche. Maude later married Otto Friedrich who took over Union Mills.

valuable, Gabriel and John decided to return to Oregon and look for land to settle.

Land Ahoy!

Gabriel and John took the Schooner Montague by sea for the return trip from San Francisco to Portland. John later related the experience thus: (Budget, 1897)

"The vessel was a fore and aft schooner of about 500 tons and was called the George H. Montague. Her commander and owner was Captain Montague, a typical Yankee skipper, a born sailor and a prodigy in the use of an unlimited vocabulary of oaths.

"A cargo of general merchandise was taken on and with eight cabin passengers and about twenty in the steerage the schooner set sail from San Francisco on January 1, 1851. A very pretty run made up the coast and just before dark on the evening of January 4, we hove in sight of the Columbia, where Captain Coates, a Hudson Bay Company pilot, and the one who lost the ship Peacock on Peacock spit, was taken on board.

"A stiff gale was blowing and the heavy seas were breaking over the then dangerous bar until it resembled a boiling cauldron of seething waters. To cross in was impossible, and the little vessel was put out to sea. The storm continued for eighteen days, but during that time we sighted the river twice each day. The sails were torn into shreds, and when at last we were able to reach port there was scarcely a whole piece of canvas on the vessel. We were not driven any distance northward, but remained almost opposite the Columbia during the whole time.

"On the evening of January 22, the bar had moderated somewhat, and shortly after sundown pilot Coates headed the little craft for the river, bringing her safely in and dropping anchor where Sand Island now is."

Opportunities in Oregon

Upon their return, the two brothers headed for what is now called Milwaukie and built the first warehouse there. Finding that they were not always in agreement, they decided to split and go separate ways. Gabriel headed ten miles south of Oregon City to a place later to be called Union Mills and John Corse headed ten miles northwest of Oregon City to a place later to be called Lake Oswego. And the die had been cast for this family who would contribute so much to the settling of the Oregon Territory.

Union Mills Founded

On July 22, 1852, Gabriel took up a homestead along the banks of Milk Creek and established a home for himself and his bride, the former Sarah Glover of Eagle Creek. There in 1854, he built one of the Oregon

John Corse Trullinger
1828 - 1901

country's first sawmills.

Until 1890 only rough lumber was produced. In that year, Gabriel imported from England what was said to be the Pacific Coast's first power-driven planer. This piece of machinery is now in the museum of the Oregon Historical Society at Portland. It is not on display at this time.

When the planer was installed, Gabriel and Sarah had been married fifteen years and had a family of seven - Daniel Newton (b. 1853, m. Juliet Howard), James Barton (b. 1856, m. Nealie Rowell), Edward L. (b. 1861, m. Mary Martin), Dellazon Lee (b. 1863, m. Maude Paine), Sara Ellen (b. 1865, m. Edward Paine), Jane Elizabeth (b. 1867, m. Frank Paine), and Isaac V. (b. 1869, m. Elizabeth Crowley). Two other children passed away. The oldest son, Ben, died in infancy and a daughter, Katherine, drowned in Milk Creek at the age of 12.

In 1877, Gabriel put water power from his Milk Creek dam to work in another mill - this to produce flour. (Howard's Mill in Mulino was already in existence.) Trullinger's mill had steel rollers, not stone, and produced white flour, bran, shorts, middlings and a product similar to cream of wheat.

In 1879, a third mill for wool processing was added. Wool from the rural area's sheep was washed and carded, bound for home spinners who spun their own yarn and knitted garments for their families.

With these three mills in production, Gabriel gave the name Union Mills to his operations. Machinery for all three Trullinger mills was brought by ship across the Atlantic, around Cape Horn and up the Pacific coast. It was then hauled by wagon from Oregon City to Union Mills.

Another Trullinger family enterprise was a hop yard operated by Edward from 1880 until 1900. Hops were dried, baled and warehoused at Union Mills until Ed moved to Eagle Creek.

Isaac Trullinger built a water-powered furniture factory upstream from Union Mills and manufactured solid oak household furniture. Some of his products are still in the family. His mill was up the present Windy City Road, and utilized power from a dam Isaac built in the creek.

Woodworking was a favorite of Daniel Newton Trullinger. He built and ran a factory to turn out handles for axes and other tools. His liking for wood led him to make a checkerboard, inlaid from wood taken from the covered wagon that had brought his grandparents over the Oregon Trail.

Water provided power for the Union Mills sawmill until 1886, when a steam boiler was installed.

John Corse Trullinger
Lake Oswego and Astoria

Meanwhile, Gabriel's younger brother, John Corse Trullinger, was busily stamping out his place in history ten miles northwest of Oregon City.

John Corse would go on to be a great promoter, inventor and politician.

He married Hannah Boyle in 1853 and they had six sons and two daughters. They were Elizabeth Ann (dob. unknown, m. W. D. Mack), Isabelle S. (b. 1861, m. W. J. Barry, then Theodore T. Geer), Perry A. (dob. unknown, m. Emma Watt), Thomas O. (b. 1862, m. Agnes F. Pope), Sherman Grant (b. 1864, m. Marie Adele Sovey), Thaddeus Stevens (b. 1867, m. Georgia Badollet), John Henry (b. 1870, m. Sadie Gilbert) and William T. (b. 1872, m. Hallie Raymond).

For eleven years he operated a flour and sawmill on Fanno Creek, near Tigard. He also engaged in farming and his was the first timothy sown in Oregon.

In the early 1900s, transportation seemed to go from the horse and buggy to the automobile overnight.

In the automobile from left: Maude Trullinger, Gladys Schuebel, Blanche Trullinger and Grace Schuebel.

In the horse drawn buggy: standing is Harvey Schuebel, seated from left: Otto Friedrich, Blanche Trullinger, Grace Schuebel and Maude Trullinger.

Dellazon L. Trullinger
ca. 1885

Maude Paine Trullinger
ca. 1885

When John heard that a place called Oswego might be building an iron foundry he felt that profitable ventures would reside in that area. A donation land claim had already been filed by A. A. Durham. He had laid out a town site and named it in honor of his home town, Oswego, New York. In 1865, John Corse bought the town site, improved the Durham Sawmill and renamed it Oswego Milling Company.

The first iron produced west of the Rocky Mountains was cast at Oregon Iron Company in Oswego on August 24, 1867. John took the first two pigs cast and planned to use them as street markers at his Oswego town site. Today, one is at the Oregon Historical Society (not on display) and the other is in Lake Oswego. Today Oregon's first iron smelter may be seen at George Rogers Park in Lake Oswego near the boat ramp.

He next founded a business called People's Transportation Company with the dream that it would transport the abundant produce grown in the Tualatin Valley and other goods between Portland and Hillsboro. He ran an extensive towing and boating business with his seventy one foot steam scow named "Minnehaha."

In 1869, he sold his Oswego interests and moved to Forest Grove. An excerpt from "Oregon Native Son" tells us more of John's accomplishments:

"Placing his children in school at Forest Grove, he went to Boston, where he built a turbine water-wheel, and going to Lowell, to Emerson's water-wheel testing works, he had his wheel tested, and succeeded in obtaining from it seventy six percent of working power. Having bought the Centerville flouring and saw mills, near Forest Grove, of Ulysses Jackson, he operated them until 1877, when they were burned. In 1875, he bought property in Astoria, where he subsequently built the West Shore mills, the

Maude & Dellazon Trullinger in their elder years.

property covering twelve acres, and containing, besides the mills, warehouses, wharves, barns and electric light station. During his experience in the lumbering business he built, on the Walluskie Creek, three and one-half miles of the standard-gauge railway track, with fifty-six pound rails, and employed about 150 men.

"In December, 1885, he commenced the construction of an electric light plant in Astoria, from which the city is lighted. Mr. Trullinger has held various offices of public trust in Astoria and Clatsop County. He was mayor of Astoria from 1886 to 1888, and previous to that was a member of the city council. In December, 1891, he was elected president of the board of police commissioners. In June, 1892, he was elected by a large majority to the state legislature. He was one of the organizers of the Republican party in Oregon in 1856."

Daniel Perry Trullinger
'Boy Bridge Builder"

Gabriel's younger brother, Daniel Perry, who was only eight years old when the family arrived in Oregon, would grow up to be a bridge builder, politician, owner of sawmills and a flour mill.

In 1872, he was united in marriage to Emily Wood and they had at least three children; Frederick L. (b. 1874, m. Grace Fox), Carl S. (b. 1875, m. Alice Laughlin), and Mary (b. 1880, m. A. Fred Henry).

"The Centennial History of Oregon" relates Daniel Perry's story:

"He began earning his own livelihood at the early age of fourteen, working on a farm for two years. Subsequently he learned the trade of a millwright and carpenter under the direction of his brother and his work along that line included the building of bridges. He was awarded the contract for and superintended the construction of the second upper Clackamas bridge, which was built exclusively of wood and spanned one hundred and twenty feet. At that time he was known as the "boy bridge builder." In 1863, in association with a brother, he built the old Oswego sawmill but sold his interest therein at the end of a year. He next attended school at Portland, Oregon, for three winter seasons and later spent a year as a student at Forest Grove, Oregon. Mr. Trullinger then devoted another year in the construction of bridges and on the expiration of that period returned to Oswego, where he again operated the sawmill in partnership with his brother for two years. In 1868, he was elected to the legislature on the Republican ticket and ably served his constituents for one term. After leaving the general assembly he became superintendent of Ben Halladay's sawmill, acting in that capacity for three years. He then operated a sawmill for his brother for one year and superintended the operation of the Weidler sawmill for two years. In 1875, he purchased a flour mill at North Yamhill and has operated the same continuously since with the exception of two years, during which period he built four sawmills for different companies. He owns a tract of land comprising fifteen acres and also has a handsome residence in Yamhill."

This generation of Trullingers had added much to the settling of the great Oregon Territory.

Turn of the Century

The turn of the century arrived at Union Mills. Gabriel had aged and his son, Dellazon, had taken over the reins of management at Union Mills.

In the late 1800s, Dellazon married Maude Paine. They had four children: Blanche, Maude, Pauline and a son, Grant. Dellazon and Maude built the large, gracious, four bedroom white house that still compliments Union Mills today.

May of 1901, tragedy struck the Trullinger family at Union Mills. The family kept a boat at the Old Lake to cross on, but for unknown reasons, that day Grant, age fourteen, had decided to try to cross on the logs. He fell into the lake and drowned, leaving Dellazon without a son to carry on the Trullinger name.

In 1906, Gabriel Trullinger died and the mill operations were taken over by Del. He had been helping his father since the age of 15.

A new modern sawmill was built a short distance from the old sawmill in 1907. A new dam in Milk Creek was also built about that time. Logs were kept in the mill-pond and sawed as needed. This mill had two planers and two steam engines. The sawdust, shavings and slab wood

were burned in the ovens that produced the steam in the boilers that powered the stationary steam engines.

Much of the lumber was sold locally but some was hauled by wagon to Liberal and loaded on rail cars for shipment. The products produced in the flour mill were mostly sold locally and some of the flour was hauled to Oregon City and Molalla.

1912 Flood Damaging

About 1912, there was a heavy flood in the area and Milk Creek went on a rampage. Many buildings along its path were damaged. The flour mill was moved about fifteen feet from its foundation and had to be moved back and set level again. In the early days, Milk Creek was used to move the logs that were cut along the banks and then floated downstream to be sawed. Logs were cut along the creek, all the way to Colton and floated down to the sawmill during periods of high water. Many oldtimers told of harried experiences they had while floating logs down the creek during these periods of high water. They rode the logs with a pike-pole in their hands, keeping the logs in the main flow of the creek.

Horse Logging Began

After 1905, most of the logging was done with horses. Logs cut on the hill were dumped in the Old Lake and pulled to the brink of the hill with a donkey engine and then shot down the chute to the mill pond.

Later a new lake was made for log storage. It is still here and many homes have been built around its shores. Logs were pulled by horse teams from the new lake to the Old Lake.

The Trullinger home was the scene of many social functions in the early 1900s. This is the wedding party of Art Zwiefel and Pauline Trullinger. Maude and Otto Friedrich are on the far left. Grover Friedrich and Blanche Trullinger on the right.

The Trullinger and Schuebel girls were cousins. Left to right: Blanche Trullinger, Gladys Schuebel, Maude Trullinger, Grace Schuebel and Pauline Trullinger. ca. 1915

1900s Age of
Home Social Functions

The early 1900s were the age of home social functions. Once the Trullinger girls became teenagers the big white house at Union Mills was often filled with young people having a good time.

The Friedrich name entered the picture when Maude Trullinger married Otto Friedrich in 1914. The Molalla Pioneer described the wedding:

"A very pretty wedding was solemnized Wednesday, June 17, at the home of D. L. Trullinger when his daughter, Miss Maude became the wife of Mr. Otto Friedrich of Molalla. Miss Blanche Trullinger, sister of the bride, acted as bridesmaid and Mr. Mark Hungate was best man. The bride wore silk crepe de chine with draperies of shadow lace and carnations with asparagus ferns. The bridesmaid wore blue messaline and carried pink carnations. The house was tastily decorated with orange blossoms and red roses, intermingled with ferns. Friends and relatives numbering about fifty were present. Immediately after the ceremony, which was officiated by Rev. S. E. Witty, a wedding breakfast was served. Mr. and Mrs. Otto Friedrich left at 3 p.m. on an extended tour through California, after which they will make their home in Molalla."

Feed Mixing
Business Begins

During the 1920s, the feed mixing and manufacturing business came into being. Union Mills installed a hammer mill feed grinder and a feed mixer about 1928. They were both run by water power as was the flour mill.

Flour manufacture was discontinued about 1940 as the feed business expanded. More modern flour mills developed, rendering the old flour mill machinery obsolete. Union Mills has always kept up with the times in poultry and animal feed manufacture. During the 1950s Union Mills purchased a pellet mill and began operating a bulk feed truck.

Mark Hungate operated the flour mill for many years. Otto Friedrich took over operation of the flour and feed mill about 1932 and the sawmill in 1935. The sawmill ceased operation in 1940. The flour mill ceased operation in 1941 and became a total feed mill.

Ken and Alvin Friedrich, Otto and Maude's sons, took over operation of the flour and feed mill in 1939. (Otto and Maude also had a daughter, Dolores.) The brand was "UM" feeds. Prior to that it was "Table Loaf." In 1941, a heavy flood washed out the mill dam and the mill was converted to diesel power and later to electricity.

After Ken and Alvin retired, Ken's son Bob took over the Union Mill operation.

*   *   *

Friedrich Bros. Creamery and Ice Works operated in Molalla from 1908 to 1913. The business was operated by Frank and Otto Friedrich, who were set up in business by their father, Bernhard Friedrich. ca. 1910. *Photo courtesy of the Molalla Historical Society.*

CHAPTER VIII

The Bagbys of Wilhoit

PART ONE: "The Bagbys"   . by Mary Bagby Walling as told to Fred Lockley

PART TWO: "The Hunter of the Old West" . . . . by John Bagby

Bagby Hot Springs

A much treasured experience is a warm soak in the hollowed cedar logs of Bagby Hot Springs. One pulls the little wooden plug to let the 136 degree mineral water flow into the tub from a wooden trough and then totes buckets of cold water to cool the bath before entering. Some soak in the nude in the private bath houses, but most wear bathing suits while listening to the music of the forest birds and watching the chipmunks scurry about from a front row forest-seat in the tub.

The Springs are located in the rustic wilderness of Mt. Hood National Forest 60 miles east of Portland, Oregon via Highway 224. They are reached by a 1 1/2 mile walk down a trail through the woods. In 1876, the Springs namesake, Robert Bagby, came upon a board with an inscription that said "Run boys, hell's not 300 feet from here." He soon discovered that puff of steam over yonder was only hot mineral water.

Today the Springs are operated by The Friends of Bagby Hot Springs, a non-profit organization dedicated to the preservation, restoration and operation of this historic natural resource.

Bibliography:
Bagby, John, Personal Diary, dated 1905
Lockley, Fred, Bagby History as told by Mary Bagby Walling, <u>Oregon Journal</u>, 1915
Lynch, Vera M., "Recreational Facilities," <u>Free Land for Free Men</u>, 1973

PART ONE:

"The Bagbys"

by Mary Bagby Walling as told to Fred Lockley

"A picture of family life of the early days in Oregon at that life's best - and that was mighty good - is drawn for Mr. Lockley by one who lived it as one of a family of 18 persons who dwelt in peace and plenty that one and all worked for and didn't begrudge the work at that.

"Mary Bagby Walling lives at Rockaway, on the Oregon

The William Bagby Family. Mid 1890s. The family lived on a donation land claim southeast of Molalla. Front row, left to right: John, Grandma Harriet, Grandpa William, and Mary (Walling). Middle row, left to right: Alice (Sandford), Calvin, Flora (Jarisch), Margaret (Pelkey), Eliza (Hamilton), Robert. Back row, left to right: Frank, Edward, Henry, Jesse. *Photo courtesy of Wilma Novak.*

Coast, in Tillamook County. I sat in her immaculate parlor a day or so ago while she brought before my mental vision vivid pictures of the past.

"I was born a Bagby," said Mrs. Walling, "and I was christened Mary. I was born on my parents' donation land claim four miles southeast of Molalla, March 30, 1859. There were 16 children in our family, of which I was the sixth. My father, who was a blacksmith and millwright, was born in Springfield, Ill., 101 years ago. My mother, whose maiden name was Harriet Macauley, was born at Glasgow, Scotland, in 1830. She came to America with her parents when she was 9 years old. Her father was an expert weaver, being particularly good at silk weaving. When a shawl was to be woven for the young Victoria when she was newly crowned queen of England, Grandfather Macauley was selected to weave it. My mother was 18, or nearly so, when she married my father, in 1848. She was 22 when they started across the plains by ox team and prairie schooner for the far off and far-famed Willamette Valley in Oregon in the spring of 1853. She then had three children, the oldest of whom was not yet 3. Robert was nearly 3, John was a tiny toddler, and Calvin was 3 months old. The Indians stampeded their work cattle, the cholera broke out in their train, and they had to stop repeatedly to dig shallow graves beside the Oregon Trail to bury victims of the scourge that took such a heavy toll of the emigrants on the plains that year.

"They reached Oregon City in the late fall of that year, and father rented a log cabin on the Clackamas for the family while he spent the winter working in a sawmill. Like most of the Oregon pioneers, father was a hunter; so he usually had a deer hanging up on the shed for mother's use. Mother cooked deer meat in an iron pot in the fireplace and baked her bread in a Dutch oven; for that was before stoves were in common use.

"In the spring of 1853 father took up a square mile of land four miles southeast of Molalla. When I was 6, I did my share of the work. I used to stand on a box to wash the dishes. I never remember seeing mother when she was not busy cooking, nursing the children, washing or ironing. She saved the ashes and the grease and made all the soap we used. She washed the wool from the sheep we raised, carded it, spun the thread, dyed it with oak bark or with black walnut hulls or made it blue with indigo, wove it, and made linsey-woolsey dresses for us girls or suits for the boys. She made butter and cheese, and from the deerskins that father tanned she made buckskin gloves and trousers, which she sold to the men in the harvest crews roundabout. The boys would catch lots of salmon below the falls at Oregon City, or trout in the nearby streams. Mother would usually put up two or three barrels of salted salmon and salted trout for winter use. She also dried the deer hams for jerked venison, to be used in winter.

"When father would come home from his work we would all have supper, and while the girls were washing the dishes mother would get out her mending basket and father would get out his kit of shoemaker tools and they would work by the light of a whale oil lamp or by candlelight, till bedtime. Father made and kept in repair the shoes for mother and himself and their 16 children; so there was usually some work to be done of an evening with his kit of tools.

"We raised plenty of potatoes, turnips, carrots, beets, cabbages and fruit, as well as chickens, sheep, pigs and cattle. These, with trout and salmon, deer meat and wild birds - pheasants, grouse and ducks - supplied us with plenty of wholesome food. We children picked enough hazel nuts to last through the winter. We also pared apples in great quantity, which we dried for use as apple sauce or for apple pies during the winter. We also put up plenty of apple butter. Father usually put up a few barrels of cider, and of course we made our own vinegar.

"Occasionally we went to house-raisings, barn-raisings, quilting bees, log rollings and country dances. Father was a good hand with the fiddle; so he furnished the music for neighborhood dances. We children played post-office and other kissing games. There were nine boys and seven girls in our family. Twelve of these 16 children lived to maturity. Three of my brothers are bachelors. Ten of us are still living. My brother John, who is 75 lives here in Rockaway. My brother Robert lives at Oswego, near Portland. Calvin, who is a contractor and builder, lives at Oregon City. Henry is running a hotel at Klamath Falls. Edward is a farmer in California. Margaret married Richard Pelkey. She lives at Molalla. Eliza married Jim Hamilton, a lumberman. They live at Wheeler. Flora married P. H. Jarisch. He is a nurseryman. They live in Oswego. Jesse is farming the old place, near Molalla, that father took up in 1853.

"In 1882 I was married to A. G. Walling, a widower with two children. Elder William Dart performed the marriage ceremony. I moved as a bride to my husband's nursery, four miles north of Oregon City, near Oswego. We lived there for the next 25 years. When our children had left the home next we moved to Rockaway. This was before the railroad was built. When we built our home there was only one house here - that of F. P. Miller. We have seen Rockaway build up from two houses to a growing and prosperous summer resort."

*   *   *

PART TWO:

"The Hunter of the Old West"

by John Bagby

Reprinted from a book of hand-written stories by John Bagby dated 1905. Several men claim to have discovered Wilhoit Springs and John Bagby is one. He refers to Wilhoit Springs as the soda springs.

"I was born in Illanois Medorma Co. crossed the plains with my father and mother in 1852. My father settled for the winter 5 miles of Oregon City. The next spring moved to the old donation claim 20 miles south of Oregon City, where we have resided up to the present time. My father had just finished our log cabin all but putting in the fireplace and we had moved in and after we had all gone to bed a large cougar walked up and serveyed us and the new log cabin through the square we had left for a fireplace. The gun was not in reach of father so we lay quiet and the cougar went on past and we did not see him anymore. I shall first try to tell you the names of diferent animals that roamed this wildreness of the west. They are the brown and black and cinamon bear, the cougar, wildcat, lynx, large timber wolf, coyote or prairie wolf, martin, beaver, fisher ottar, mink, muskrat. The elk and deer and Spanish and wild cattle. A few other small animals not worth mentioning. The diferent animals I have spoken of could be seen in the day time as they was very numerous, father then procedded to clear land and plant fruit trees. And the deer would come in at night and eat the young fruit trees, and father would take the gun and mother the pich torch and shine there eyes and father would that way kill plenty of deer and keep up plenty fully supplied with meat. My father learned me to shoot and handle a gun at a very early age as he was away from home to work a good deal. and my mother and I always took the gun with us when we went blackberrying as father told us it was best, and mother would carry the gun as I was small. And we did not know but we would run on a bear as they like berrys too and one time we started blackberrying and a bear walked up on a log and mother got afraid and would not shoot at him or let me shoot so we had to go home without any berys that day and

John Bagby with his dog "Snap"
Photo courtesy of Wilma Novak.

another time we met an old rattle snake and mother shot him so we did not pick any berys that time. I think it was the 2nd year after we went on the place the Indians was thought to be on the war path. The Indians sent Indian Peter to spy and see how the whites were armed and the whites told Peter there guns shoot a long ways and for him to tell the Indians that there bows and arrows was no good and so the Indians did not break out as the whites all forted up at Wilhoits fourt about a week and every one then went home and there was no troble. I was the discoverer of the famous soda spring which took its name after this same man named Wilhoit which name it bears to this day. At about ten years of age I shot my first wild cat and my brother Robert a year or two younger than I drug home our prize witch I thought was something grand and so did father and mother. On my next hunt I shot a deer and then I thought I was a hunter indeed. After that I did nothing else much but hunt the wild animals of the woods and everytime I did go hunting I would go a little farther away. That is how I found this great soda springs. Which is now a grand sumer resort. I am 55 years old, never was out of the state of Oregon since I crossed the plains. Summered one summer in eastern Oregon as a sheep herder. The rest of my life has been on the old donation claim with my father and mother in the foothills of the Cascade Mountain . One day I went out to hunt the cow with gun and dogs and found where a bear had been using on a cow that had mired in the swamp near our place. John Cline had told me if I found any sign of Brnin to let him know and he would bring his dogs an we would capture him. So John Cline and Ed Ogle, my father and I started out in persuit. We followed on the trail about three miles, when we found her and four cubs, two black ones and two brown ones. just before we came upon her, my father, Ed Ogle and Jake Cline got discouraged and turned back I proposed to stay with them till we got them; so John Cline said he would stay with me, she had whiped her cubs up a stump and went on to draw us away from the cubs. John Cline ventured in with gun in hand to get a shot. The rest of the party came up on hearing our shot. Then father ventured up to see if he could get a shot, she took after the dogs and father fell off the log. Here came the old bear almost over my father where he had fallen. God Almighty; she'll catch me, I heard my father exclaim. So I began to think something must be done. As none of the others started, I made a break and I soon settled the bear with a bullet between the eyes. When I came out of the brush, where I had shot the old bear I found Ed Ogle and Jake Cline up a tree so I went on down where the cubs were. There was a large wild cherry tree beside the stump so I climed up where the cubs were holding on to the cherry tree and told the men to cach the cubs as I threw them down. One of the little cubs would keep backing down the stump and John Cline said you little devil, I'll shoot you if you don't stay up there and give him a shot which just struck him in the ball of the foot and he went up and stayed John Cline said he would take one for a pet and I took one for a pet. The other men said they did not want any pet bears. Then we started back home. Before we had gone a half mile we concluded we did not want any pet bears eather for our hands were scrached and bleeding. So we killed and skined them and took the skins and also had plenty of bear meat to take home also. I think it was the next year

after finding the soda springs I took watch my little hunting dog, a brindle bob tailed dog with me and was about a half mile south of soda when we routed what I suposed was a band of wild cattle. Which afterwards proved to be a band of elk. I followed on the trail untill I came in sight of them but could not get a shot I went on till night and camped on a creek named Beaver Creek. Early next morning I started on the trail again. About half mile and they had all gone in a big swamp. So I thought best go on ahead of them. Then I sent Watch back to drive them to me but they did not come out where I supposed they would and he got after one in about half an hour and went clear out of hearing so I waited a while to see if he would bring him back after while I heard my old faithfull dog coming back so I got on a high log and did not have to wait long till here came a large animal he came in about 60 yds of me on a sweeping trot with old Watch at his heels. I throwed the gun up to my face and as he came in the sights I fired. Took him in the heart and he wheeled on the dog for a fight. But he reeled and fell. I went down to see what he was. I had never seen an elk before and discovered it was nothing of the cattle kind and knew it must be an elk. So I went to work and skined him. This was late in the afternoon and I started for home and dark came on so I camped, cooked my supper of elk meat and took the heart in my travel sack to carry home. The second night I camped out again and early in the next morning I started for home. When I got home it was bout 8 o'clock. The neighbors was almost ready to go and hunt me I heard them talking. My uncle said if John is not here by 9 o'clock we will go and see if we can find him. And steped in the door, my uncle said Where have you been all this time? I was away back of the soda springs at what is known now as high hill where I had killed this noble animal. I took off my pack sack and laid it on the table. My uncle asked me what I had. I told him to look and see. When he took the heart out he said to my father. He has killed one of them wild cattle. No it is not any of the wild cattle I said. They asked me what kind of horns it had I told them its horns were 14 to 15 inches long and began to fork at the top. Then they asked me what kind of tail it had. I told them it had a tail 4 or 5 inches long. Then they wanted to know what color it was. I told them around the neck and head it was almost black but the hair on the body was a light yellow color. I remember what my uncle said. He had killed an elk. He said. They wanted to know if I could take them to the place where I had killed it. I told them yes and mother said, I will get Johny some breakfast as he has been out two days and two nights and must be hungry. I had had nothing to eat but elk meat all the time I was gone. I finished my breakfast and by that time they was ready to go so as we started I told them I had looked out a better way to go with the horses than to go away around by the soda springs. So I led the way. they following. After I got a round to the place where Wm Maringo now lives they asked them if I could show them from there where I killed the elk and I pointed and showed them high hill and told them at the foot of that mountain.

How will we ever get the horses there they said. I told them to follow me and we would get there. They looked astonished my uncle said, you don't mean today. You killed it away at the foot of that high mountain yes that is the place. Well lets be a moving then they said. So I led on and we got there Was you not afraid to go so far? said my uncle. No white man has been here before till you. It is a great wonder you did not get lost. We never would have come here to find you. I wa about 16 years old when I killed this elk and this wa my first one. so we went to work to cutting up the elk meat and we did not carry many bones home. We loaded two horses with elk meat and had three riding horses and started for home. In about a week I went back thinking some bear or wild animal would be using on the remains of the carcas. And I was not disapointed. I seen a big bear track and began to look around and I seen some black object moving in the fern and I stood looking and he walked aound and climed on a log and looked down where I was standing near the carcas.

He did not look long till he got a bullet and tumbled down off the log. I camped and next morning took in a bear skin after that I went there often to hunt. It was a good place for traping beaver and I caught many a beaver there. and for three or four years I kept Beaver creek a secrete hunting and trapping ground. So I found where a bear was using on a berry patch so I took gun and dogs and started to watch for the bear. When I got in about a hundred yds of the berry patch I heard a terable racket in the bushes. I suposed it was the bear and slipped up quietly as I could. Every little bit the noise would stop and then when it would start again I would move up again. So I finely concluded it was two bucks fighting as I could hear the clash of there horns. It was not long till one whiped the other and here they both came right out where I was standing. And I was ready for him and he was so close I shot without taking sight At the crack of the gun he fell. The other wheeled and ran back in the brush. I set the gun against a tree and took out my butcher knife to cut his throat. Just as I was about to take hold of his horns he sprang to his feet and I turned and ran for my life toward the brush where he had come out. I found he

was gaining on me and I felt his horns almost touching my back. I caught hold of a small sapling and swung myself around just in time and he was running so fast he ran on past me about 20 feet and turned around. His hair all turned the rong way so I kept my eye on him for fear of another atact until I worked my way back to my gun.

I loaded up the gun and went back where I could see him and broke his neck. My Father said What do you say John we saddle the horses and ride up to the butte. Which is the place between Ed Carter place and George Wingfield. Why it wa called by that name I do not know. So I told him alright. We rode up there and hitched our horses. Father said he would not go far away from the horses. He asked me where I was going to hunt. I said, I'm gong over in the green timber I think the deer are there the dogs started a wounded deer. The deer ran around in a circle. I did not know it was wounded and pretty soon they caught it. But just before they started it I saw a mans track. So while I was standing listening when I heard a noise to my right. Then I turned my head and looked but did not see anything at first. Then I listened for the dogs and I heard a faint noise of them and I concluded they had caught the deer. Then when I looked again where I had first heard the noise down in the gulch. I could see the deers feet. I supposed it was man coming up out of the gulch. Then my attention was turned to the dog again. When I looked again a large cougar was standing at the edge of the gulch with a deer in his mouth. I was standing with the gun on my shoulder when he caught my movement he dropped the deer and was in the gulch out of sight in a moment. I got my gun ready and waited to see if he would come back after his meat but he did not come back and I went to where the dogs had the deer. I got old Watch and the other two dogs would not follow me so I left them with the deer. I went back to where the cougar had dropped the deer and old Watch took the track. He went about a hundred yds and he lost the track and when I come up with him, he was circling round trying to find the track agan. There was two big trees and one had fell across the other and the cougar had sprung up on the uper log and that was what fooled old Watch. So I called him down to where the logs crossed and when he got on the dog he seen the cougar and began to bark and jumped down on the cougar and then the fight began and soon the other two dogs came and then they was to much for Mr. cougar, and he took to his heels and made for a big green cedar tree and you bet he had to clime. The gun I was hunting with was an old Kentucky rifle a muzzle loader of small calabre. Just took onebuck shot I went up to where he was treed and took off the old cap and put on a new one.

I raised the gun and fired as he would not keep his head still I shot at his brest. He fell at the foot of the tree and all three dogs bounded on him. But they did not hold him as he sprang away from them and came bounding at me. I raised the gun to strike him and I seen he was not near enough so I took refuge behind a tree. He passed on and jumped on a log and run fifty or so feet on the log and turned and come back on another log towards me again. I had no time to load the gun so I pulled out my dirk knife my father had given me and prepared myself for him but when he made the last spring off the log I seen then he was blind from the shot I had given him and he fell dead. So I skined him and went back to where father and the horses were. and father had gone home and left me. So I had two deer and a cougar to take home. The cougar measured 9 feet and 11 inches from the end of the nose to tip of tail. I went on home then and one of the neighbors was there, Mr. Sawtell. He was the man that measured the cougar and he was largest I had ever killed but I had killed in all 2 cougars after I got home I had a good supper of venison and I took one of the cougar toushes and made a charger. To load my gun. So this ends the cougar hunt.

And when I took the elk horns to Mr. Galeman of Portland I took down 100 pounds of dried elk meat and sold it for 20 cts a pound: Willie Thomas old man, Dart and myself, went elk hunting went about 7 miles beyond table rock; to my old camping ground. We got there in the evening in time to take a little hunt, after we got our dinner we all loaded our guns and started out to see if we could see any elk tracks. When we had gone about a 1/2 mile, we found where there had been some elk. They asked me where do you think we will find them. I pointed where I thought they were, and old Sulivan started. He thought I meant for him. It was not long untill he was running after two elk. He did not run too far untill they seperated. One of them run up on top of Laurelhill and there he stoped for fight, the dog still barking at him. I did not follow the way the dog and elk went but took a cut off and came in under the hillside so he could not see me. I worked my way causiously up the hillside untill I came within forty steps of him. Then I could see the elk. A tree had fell up the hill, the elk was on the other side of the log and I shot him through the heart. He gave a bunt and fell, started to roll. I thought he was going to roll over the hill where I was, but a log caught him: and to make shure I give me another shot in the back of the head. In a few minits old man Dart and Willie Thomas came up. We skined the elk and quarted him up and hung them up to cool and went to camp. It was getting dark now. So early next morning

we came after the meat, and took it back to camp and I proceded to make a rack to hang it up to dry: When we got the meat dried the old man Dart wanted to come home. He said if I would take him back to green camp, he thought he could come home from there alone. In coming back, I seen where a large elk had crssed the trail. I told old man Dart I'll have him before 10 oclock tomorrow: So Willie and I went back to hunt awhile longer, and followed this elk track untill we seen he was going down in a little cave. I told Willie we would go around on the other side of the cave, and come in from the opposite direction, so that he would not find us out. When we got in the cave we could hear him, he was horning an old rotten log; he heard us coming and went down 60 or 70 rods in a ravine to hide from us, but we followed untill we seen he was turning back on the trail that went on through. I run back but he had got by and so I turned old Sulivan loose. He run right on him and he turned to fight and Willie wanted to kill the elk, so I told him to go and follow the trail and get up close as you can. Be shure you give him a dead shot. He had not got where he could see the elk when he turned off and in running through the brush he blinded his eyes so he could not see to shoot. I began to think something was wrong as I did not hear him shoot. I knew the elk would not stay there very much longer, so I went to where I could see an open where the trail went through, so if the elk did start it would give me a chance to get a shot. I just got there in time when the elk started to run. When he got in to this open place I give him a shot breaking his hip. He turned and went down hill to a creek called Green Campcreek. When he got there he fell across the creek so I followed on down to where the dogs and elk was. The elk was not quite dead. I could hear the dogs barking and came to them. While I was there I heard Willie hollering for me and I answered him and finely he came to where I was, with both eyes badly hurt, could hardly see his way. Soon as I looked at him I said what is the matter with your eyes Willie. In going around and watching for the elk a brush hit him in the eyes he said and blinded him so bad he could not see the elk or nothing else. So we skinned the elk and carried on our backs the elk and carried it on our back up to Green Camp. It was rough country and we could not get horses in there. We stayed and dried the meat then came on home. I told Willie if he would carry the elk horns out he could have them and he has them yet. I think it was two or three years after our first elk hunt that Willie Thomas and I went for another elk hunt. We camped in about 2 miles of the hunting ground, we eat our breakfast and started early the next morning. When we got about half mile of the place where I thought we would find the game, when we heard an elk bray. I told Willie he was traveling and we would got on quietly, and maby we would meet him, so we went on untill we heard him bray again. I said Wille you stay there, and keep the dogs. I will slip over to a swamp that I knew of where I think I will find him. When I got in aobut 100 yds of the swamp, I could see him. He was horning at a big bunch of alders just tearing the bark off. I could just see through the brush a small space of his hide where his heart was, so I shot him through the heart. At the crack of the gun he wheeled around and fell dead. There were 10 more elk there and were all lying down when he fell so close to them, they all sprung up and came running right towards me and I shot another, a big cow elk. The rest of the band went on. On the dogs hearing my second shot, Willie could not hold them and here they come. Old Sulivan went on down where I shot the buck elk, and

brought a small calf out and by that time Willie was in about 60 yds of me. I hollored look out there is one coming and it stoped and Willie gave it a shot and it fell dead. We moved camp to where we killed the elk and proceded to take care and dry out meat as I never kill anymore than I could take care of and would never waste it. The 2nd night about 8 oclock in the evening we heard a distant howl of a wolf and another answering howl until there were four or 5 howling. Then they quit howling as they had all gathered together. At about 9 oclock they came close to the camp and howled and roard till it was most definng and was the most hedious noise I ever heard. Old Sulivan and Queen our dogs had to be tied up to keep them at camp. As the wolves would have got them off in the dark they would have eaten the dogs. Just before daylight the wolves came around our camp again and set up there unearthy yells and Willie as it grew lighter

An early hunting party. The Mitts family from left: Melvin, Ed, Jim, Lewis, Frank and Jess. Photo taken near Myrtle Point, Oregon. The Mitts family was from the Needy area. *Photo courtesy of Molalla Historical Society.*

took his gun and thought he would get a shot at them and was going along and about a 100 yds from camp he saw a black object and what he thought was a black stump. And he got in forty or 50 steps of it, and it droped down and run away. It proved to be a bear sitting up on its hind legs. so he came back to camp, and he wanted me to take the dogs and see if we could get the bear. I told him no we had all the meat we could take care of and it was not the time of year for bear meat to be good so I did not want to wast meat . We stayed at this camp four days and nights, and the smae old bear came the 3rd and fourth night, and we could hear him crunching the bones and nawing on the carcas of the elk we had killed in about 50 yds of camp but we did not molest him. Willie said he wanted to name that camp so he cut a heart on a big hemlock tree and give it the name of Elkheart Swamp. The wolves did not bother us anymore. The 5th morning we sacked our meat and started for home, brought out the big elk horns and skins and I have the horns at the old home place yet. When we got about 7 miles from camp, on our road home we came into a terrible forest fire someone had let fire get away from them, and we was in a dangerous position, trees was falling around us on all sides and the fire and smoke blinded us until we had a terrible time getting through, and for a time we did not know whether we would get through or not our horses fetlocks were burned as they would break through the ground where it was a fire beneath, but we finally got through or I would not be here to tell the tale. So we went on down the trail to our homes not far away.

Thought we would without fail take a hunt again someday. I found where an old buck was staying on a creek called Cotten Branch. I had went two or three times alone to try and get him but he would always manage to get away. So I told my brother Henry if he would go with me, and take old watch and go around above maby he could drive the old buck to me. I would go down near the creek where I soposed he would cross and wait. I waited until they came on around, but they did not start the deer: While I was waiting I heard a noise down below me on the creek. I could not make out what so I told Henry we would take the dog and go, and see if we could find out what it was. We came up in about 40 steps of two big green trees standing in the thicket, old Watch cented them and away he went and out came two cougars: he run about 150 yds and comensed barking, we huried on down and he had a large cougar up a tree. I shot him and killed him and then we started into skin him and we had our backs toward the directon the cougar had come. Old Watch sprang up and began to barking and runing and I

looked and saw a cougar in about 20 feet of us, it was the mate of the one we had killed. Old Watch run him back about 40 yds and treed him. He was looking right at me.

I shot him between the eyes. I went down to the two trees and saw the cougars had killed an old buck I had been after, and had filled themselves and had been playing, was the noise that I had heard. I got the two cougars and they got the buck. We went on home, with two cougar skins. The next cougar hunt I had was on Coal Creek. I saw a cougar track in the soft dirt, it was sevrel days old, and the dogs could hardly trail it. The dogs followed on about a mile and half. Went into a cave, what I call Kirk Cove, and there they found them, three of them. The dogs run them to where there was three trees, two cougars went up one tree, and about 20 feet another tree. When I shot the first cougar, the other two came down, and run and the dogs run them about 100 yds and treed them again. I went down and shot both of them. I skined them and started out home and it was getting night on me. I met Mr. J. Offield and Mr. Blakeny on my way home and showed them the three cougar skins. I was staying with my brother Calvin Bagby near Riches sawmill. I took my gun and dogs, and started off in the woods to see if I could find any cougars. I had gone a mile and half when I struck a cougar track in the snow. I had old Queen and Sulivan. I showed them the track, they followed on till they came up on him where he had cralled under a big log where it was dry. But he did not stay there long till he had to climb a tree and I shot him right between the eyes and took his skin and went back to my brother. Next morning I went out again. I went about a mile where I killed the first cougar and the dogs started another. This was the hardest chase I ever had. They ran him clear out of hearing. I waited, did not know where they had gone till finely they brought him back to where they first started him and treed him. I made a good cougar out of him, and I had to kill him to do it. I went out hunting for deer and I killed a big buck. I took the deer home with me, but the head and horns. I wanted to save them as they were nice horns, so I layed the head and horns up on a log and thought I would come back and get them someother time. So I came back the next day to get the horns. I looked acrosss the gulch and seen a big black bear eating on the head. It was a long shot to make, he was laying length ways to me, and I aimed to shoot him between the sholders and shot to one side his back bone. He made a big bound and come running down in the gulch, and could not see him but finely he was crossihg the log and I shot him agian but did not give him a dead shot, he came on up the hill towards me, he got in 40 steps of me and just then the dogs came back from chasing a deer. The old bear stood up on his hind feet and I seen him, and so did old Sulivan and Queen and they made for him and the bear and dogs had it right there. The dogs took hold of him, and the bear had old Queen down and she was hollowing for dear life. Old Sulivan took hold of the bear, I could not shot for fear of killing my dogs so I layed the gun on a log, and got out my butcher knife but just then old Sulivan took hold of the bears hind leg and yanked him off of Queen and I could not stand to see my faithful old dogs tore up so I backed up again a fir tree, and I settled him with a bullet through the head. Just as I got him killd, Moor Dimick hollared and asked me what I was shooting at. I told him a bear. George said I'll bet five dollars it nothing but a d---- wildcat. I said alright I'll take that bet, so we went onto the barking of the dogs where we got in about 100 yds. I could see the cougar, so I showed the cougar to George and asked him if that looked like a wildcat. Oh its a cougar aint it, he said. Yes that what it is I said. I said yes but I want to go on down as close as I can. I started on and soposed he was coming behind me. I had went about 50 yds when I discovered he was not coming. I said come on George what is the matter with you. He stood there looking at the cougar, as if he was as close as he wished to be but finely come on, and we walked on down to gether untill I got to the position I could shoot from. His body was on the oposite side of the tree. I could only see his head. I aimed to shoot him between the eyes, but owing to a cartridge a man by the name of Walker had given me which was to small for my gun, thinking I would shoot it away and get rid of it. And when the dog treed the cougar I forgot to change the load and made a bad shot, hit the cougar in the mouth. The bullet struck one of his big teeth and divided the bullet and breaking the lower jaw, knocking him out of the tree. As soon as he fell George started and said he would go up and see the dogs wool it. When he looked to see the best way to go, the cougar got away from the dogs and rushed by him all most touching him. I said look out but the cougar wasfast and went under a big log that was up a foot or two from the ground. He stopped to fight the dogs, I reloded and got where I could see his body and shot him George said Ill be D--- if I want any more cougars jumping around me like that. One did, so we skined the cougar and George said we better be getting back home. Well we'll go back where the dogs started this one. There is nearly always two and mabe the dog might tree another one I said, so we went. So shure

enough the dog soon treed another in a marte maple tree and George said have you your own loading. Yes I said I only had me one bad cartridge Now you just watch and

see if you dont see the fur fly between his eyes which at the crack of the gun George said he did see the hair part for I had hit him square between the eyes. We skined him and went on home. I think that each one measured about 8 feet and 1/8. His wife said aint you glad you went with John now. George said yes. I know now what it is to hunt cougars and what they look like up a tree, so I went on down to my brothers with my two cougar skins. Well one morning George Walling, Barry Walling, Wm., Johnson, Dick Johnson and Saul Clark came up to fathers from Oswego and stayed alnight.

* * *

A man by the name of Davis that everyone called uncle Jo, had a mining claim, back near the sollid silver claim. He ask me if I would go and help him do the assessment work and I told him I would. When we got about a half mile of the noted hot springs we met Al Pasole, he had been out prospecting so uncle Jo ask him to go back and help us do the assessment work. He told him if he would we will go and have an elk hunt. Al told him allright I'll go back and help you. When we got the work done we came back near Table Rock where we intended to hunt. My old dog sullivas, winded two large buck elk about 150 yds from the trail and when I came up he was baying them. What do you think he is baying they said. I told them I thought it was elk. And would slip down and see, and for them to stay where they was, when I got down where I could see, he was baying two large buck elk: I shot and killed one of them, and the other run away. We camped for the night. The next morning we skinned the elk and brought the meat out to the dungeon, and there stoped and dried the meat. Andy Wyland use to call this the halfway house but is better known now, as the dungeon. Andy Wyland kept bees and made this place his home a part of the time. Andy Wyland sold his bees to uncle Jo Davis. Then uncle Jo sold a half intrest to me. So I stoped there all winter. It was the 17 of February when I went out to see if there was any elk. There was a deep snow and this was a great place for elks winter quarters so I told uncle Jo I would go and se if there were any elk come down the trail. I followed the trail about a half a mile and there I saw large elk tracks in the trail. He had left the trail. It was getting late in the evening, I concluded it was to late to find him, so I went back to the house. Early I went and took his track and followed on some distance, then two more came in the same trail. I went on down to the Molalla River where they had crossed. I crossed a foot log and went over. They went over in a fir thicket where briers grew and was no snow to feed. I turned to the left and went around so as not to follow the trail, and tramped the snow so if the elk shold go out that way the snow being stomped would turn them back. So I went back then and followed there tracks as to where they were but could not see them. They heard me and started out the way I had made my tracks and when they came to them they started back and circled around me and made back toward the river. I had old Sulivas with me and seeing I could not get a shot I sent him after them. He ran them down into the river and they stoped to fight, and before I could get there, they started. Two went down the river and one went up the river. Old Sulivas took after the one that went up the river. I followed on a mile, and left the river and old Sulivas brought him to bay: I came up to them, and the dog was back under a log, the elk was trying to reach him with his horns. I shot him and he droped. Then I skinned him, and tromped a road in the snow to the house, then went to packing the elk meat. In my back pack, I carried his hide and horns and he was the largest elk I ever killed. and had the largest horns. A lawyer in Portland by name of L. Galeman had told me if I would get him a nice pair of elk horns, he would give me 25 dollars for them, so I took them to him and he was well pleased with them.

After carring the meat in I took my traps, set them at the carcuss, and caught a fine fishes: In about a week I went back where I had killed the big elk, and old Sulivan winded the other two elk that had come back. I told him to go up and see what it was and I stood there listening till I heard him baying. Then I went up near where he was barking in a fir thicket. I got on a big log, here came a big buck elk, running past me about 60 yards. I give him a shot and I seen him fall, but old Sulivan still kept baying in the thicket. It was not long until out came another elk, and I shot him and he ran up in ten feet of the first and fell. I skinned and carried elk meat three days, hide and horns, in getting all of the meat to the house: Then salted the meat and then dried it. Went the next morning bright and early started to tablerock for a hunt. I was not ready as I was helping father thrash and I told them I would be along in a couple of days. So when I finished thrashing, I saddled up my pony and went to Image Camp. Image Camp was named after this image of an indian cut on a rock, soposed to be done by some indian woman who had lost her man killed by a bear killing him as the bear was pictured on his back. So I got to this camp and found them all in camp and they had killed one small bear. George Walling, Bill Johnson they wanted me to take them in the elk country. I told them I would take two. The rest of them could stay at Image Camp. So George Walling, Bill Johnson and myself, started for the elk hunt. When we got near the elk grounds, I told the men to get down off there horses and walk and keep quiet and not

The "Dungeon". Al Groshong's wife in the doorway.
Photo courtesy of the Molalla Historical Society.

talk for we was liable to run on a band of elk any minit. So we had not gone 250 yds untill we run onto 5 elk aiming to cross the trail ahead of us. They was coming up a small ravine when I first seen them. Just as I saw them they was passing behind a bluff and I shot at the hindmost elk. It was a large cow elk breaking her back, so I told George and Bill to let one hold there horses and then to run down to the edge of the bluff and they would be above the elk and could shoot down on them. So they run down and just as they got there one large elk started up the hill on the other side and George shot at him and mist. Another large elk started up the same way and he turned broad side and I hollowed for them to both fire which they did and wounded him and the elk went on and George followed after. I said to Bill to shoot that cow in the head as her back was broken with the shot I had give her and it was not long till I heard George shoot and it was not long untill I seen George coming running for dear life. He took a leap over the hillside and run to where ther was a large tree. The elk came to the brow of the hill and stoped to look for George and I hollowed to George to break his neck, so he took a rest beside the tree and fired and the elk fell. At the same time Bill Johnson was shooting at the elk that I had wounded. He had shot 5 times and he hollered and said I cant kill her. I said shoot her again and at the sixth shot he killed her. George said he saw Bill shooting the other way instead of at the cow. Bill said it might be so for he was so badly excited that he thot the elk was all around him. So we went to work to skining them. After we had got them skined we went on and struck camp where there was grass for our horses. We took some elk with us and had elk meat for our supper. So we rolled up in our blankets and lay down by the camp fire but George and Bill kept talking over the elk hunt they was so excited they could not sleep and talked so much I could not sleep but very little before they had seen these elk. They imagined they was not much larger than a deer and when they saw them with those large horns that was what excited them so, and they did not sopose an elk would turn on a hunter to fight as this one had done. Early next morning we came back to Image camp where we had left the rest of our party before we got back to camp a terable thunder storm arose, the lightening flashed and the rain fell in torrents. But we unpacked our horses and spread the elk meat out on rocks on top of the hill and the lightening struck near where we left the meat turned the meat green, and rolled a huge rock down the hill near where we was camped. It was now getting quite dark and they had all gone to bed but myself. I was waiting to blow out the candle. When someone hollowed to us from the top of the hill. They could see our campfire. This was nearly 10 oclock, the storm had ceased and I hollow back to them. I would be up there directly and when I got to the top of the hill I found it was a party of berrypickers. And I piloted them down the hill to our camp. It was old Mr. Grim and wife, Bill Dart and wife, Raul Tomas and several others, so Mrs. Dart began crying and ask me if I thought she would ever get back home. I told her yes, she said how will I ever get back up that hill, her father said, why John can ride his pony right up that hill so she seemed consoled, and said no more so I helped fix their tents and they all retired for the night. The next morn was bright and fair and everybody was happy and after breakfast packed up and come home and the berry pickers went to picking berries.

I was hunting deer over on beaver creek and found a bear den. This was in the the winter in February. The snow was about a foot deep, the bear den was on a hill side under a large log. They had dug out quite a hole under the root of the tree for there winter quarters. They had carried in winter creek and leaves and fern, to make there bed and after they go in they bank the dirt up at the hole except an air space. I went to see if there were any bear in this den. Just as I got where I could see in at this air space, I could see part of a bears head. I raised my gun to my sholder and fired and shot the bear through the head. The next thing I had to dig away the dirt so I could get the bear out of the den, then had to go half the length of my body to get hold of the bear to pull her out. I took her by the foot to pull her out when another bear came at me and struck at me with its paw. I backed out and reached for the old Remington, and waited and when I seen him, give him a bullet through the head. I suposed these two was all. And then I went in again to get the old

bear out, and another year old cub came at me and struck at me same as the first one did, so I had to get the old Remington again and shoot the other cub. I draged them all out and proceeded to skin them, they were very fat. I hung them all up on a bunch of willows and went home to my brothers. The next morning early, my brothers and I came back after the bears. I gave one of the cubs to Moor Dimick an old man living alone in the Cascade mtns, the other two I took to my brothers.

The bear hunt I am about to relate happened out in the Clackamas country when I was working at the mines known as Sollid Silver. On Sundays we would not work in the mine and Henry Russell and I would go hunting to see if we could get some kind of fresh meat. Jim Dickie would take a bucket and go to the huckleberry patch after berries. On one of these hunts we went to Deer Hill. I started a large buck and was following him when I finely lost his track and while I was trying to see which way he had went, I heard a noise across the ravine. I soposed it was the buck I had been following. The brush was very thick and I could not see what it was till finely two cubs came out in sight playing with one another like kittens. When they saw me the little fellows turned and went squiralling into the brush. On hearng the cubs cry the old mother bear came running into view and was making right for one. She run down into the gulch and jumped on a log that lay in the gulch. I took eight and fired. She rolled off of the log dead. The little cubs never showed up and I seen it was getting nearly sundown so I skined the old bear and took the skin and hams and made my way back to camp.

BEAR HUNT
One Sunday evening I went with gun and dogs to look at a mine about 2 mile away from Sollid Silver mine and had got there and I was standing looking at the mine, when old Solivan one of my faithfull old dogs began to look around and sniff the air as if he winded something. He went up the hill side a 100 yds or more and began to bark as though he had something treed and climed the hillside as fast as I could and I soon came in sight of an old bear backed up against a tree and the dog baying her. I raised my gun and it failed to go and I kep snaping cartridges till I had snaped five. The bear had seen me and started to run and the cartridge by snaping it twice went off. She did not run far till she went up through a gap in the bluff. The dog could not get out where she went so he started to go around. A cub met him as it came down a tree and he soon sent it up another tree. I went up and shot it and went around and the dog followed the blood trail and soon found the mother bear dead. It was then getting late

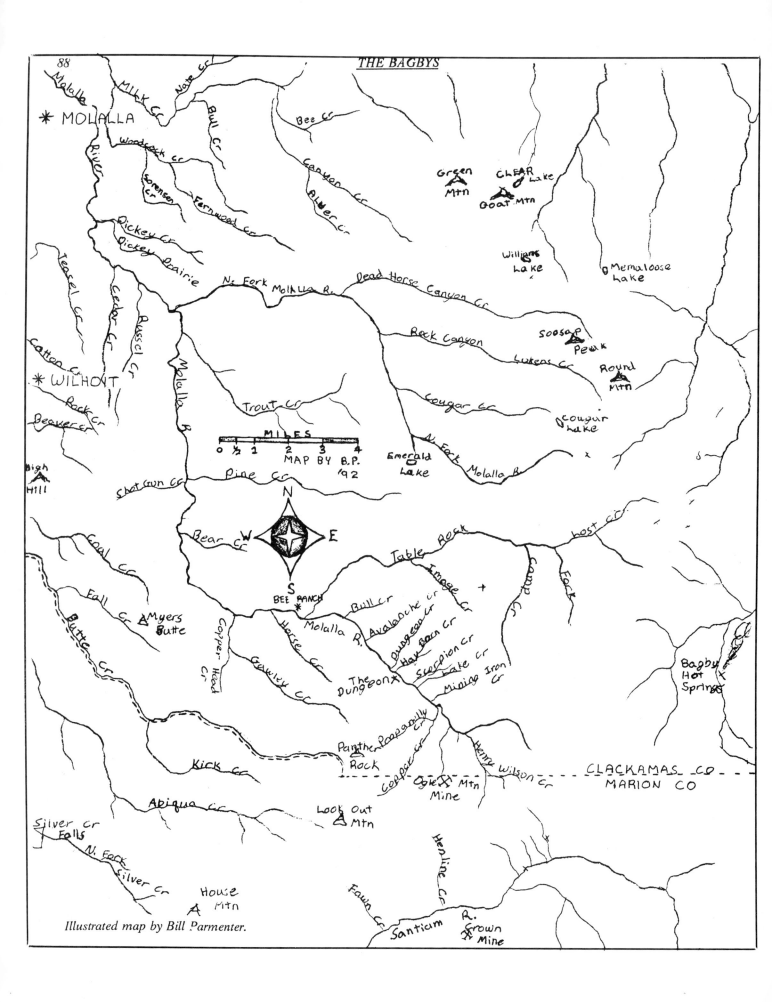

88

THE BAGBYS

Illustrated map by Bill Parmenter.

so I just took the cub into camp. The next Sunday we went over to see if the bears was in the huckleberry patch as Jim Dickie had told me there was signs of bear there. So Henry and I took our dogs old Sulivan and Dove and went. The country is open country, nothing much but huckleberry brush. The bear generly come into there feeding grounds about 4 oclock in the evening on the east side of the berry patch was a grove of timber. We came into the middle of the berry patch, so we could watch from both ways, and see the bear when they come in. While we was standing watching, I pointed toward the green timber and told Henry that was where I thought the bear would come in at and while I was telling him and pointing I saw a bear coming, and I said to Henry. There he come now. But we was to far to shoot at him. How will we manage to get close enough to kill him said Henry.

I told him we would wait, untill the bear began to feed on the berries. When he began to eat berries we kept our dogs with us, and would move up nearer. He would eat awhile and then come out and get up on a high log and look for danger. Then return to eating beries again. So we managed in this way to get up in gun shot and we was by this time close enought and the bear came out to look again and we both fired, his went and mine snaped. He fell off the log. Both dogs then made for him, he was only slightly wounded, he got old Dave down over a knotty log and the dog could not move and if it had not been for old Sulivan jerking him off would have killed old Dave. He was howling terably. The old bear went to the edge of the cliff and a tree grew down on the side of the bluff about 6 or 7 feet from the top of the cliff, he got down on the body of the tree, and Henry Russell went up and shot him in the head. We climbed over the bluff and down on a little table land, under the tree and pulled the old bear down to skin him. It was a very dangerous place as we only had barely room, to skin the bear from this little table land. It was a perpendicular cliff of 200 feet or more. We quartered the bear up and Henry would pass it up to me in this way we got our meat to the top of the cliff. We took them on our backs what we could carry in our pack sack and moved on slowly toward camp as we had to let old Dave rest every little way as he was badly hurt. The next day Al Jones and another man came into the mines and I told them where they could get all the bear meat they wanted to what we had left if they wanted to go and get it, so they went and got all the bear meat they wanted. John Cline had been out hunting and had killed a large buck. He took half the deer and hung up the other half, and he come in by my fathers place and told my brother an I if we would go and get the other half we could have it. The next morning we went to get it and when we got

there some animal had pulled it down and it had snowed since it was thare and we could not see any tracks, while we was standing and talking about what had pulled the meat down Old Watch and Tray come running in behind us and I turned to see what they was after and something passed over me just like a shadow. And the dogs was fooled and went on by the tree but soon came back, so I told Robert to go around one side of the tree, and I would go on the other side. Oh I see said Robert and it has got a big long tail. So I went around and seen what I soposed was a wild cats head. I thought Robert was excited for I thot it was a wildcat. I shot at his head as I thot and it was his foot, but it proved to be a cougar paw. I could not see it plain as it was in a cluster of small twigs. I shot him through the fore foot, and he came down out of that tree in a hurry. He stood right up on his hind feet when he came down and I did not know but he would jump on me. So I run at him with the gun and hollowed as loud as I could. He turned then and run off with the dogs after him. He ran about 50 yds and treed again, and you bet the one time I knew where his head was for I shot him right between the eyes. He was a large cougar measured about 9 feet.

My brother Robert was working for a man by the name of Albright and went out one evening to drive up the cows. He heard some kind of anamal hollowing. The noise he said was above him and all around him. He did not see the animal. The next morning old Sawtell went out to plow. He said his horses kept looking and looked and he saw a cougar crossing a little opening. It was about half way from his house to Albrights. He took his team and put them in the barn and saddled up and came for me and old Watch. I went back with him to where he last saw the cougar. I showed the dogs the track. It was not long till I heard him running. The cougar run about a mile before the dog treed him. He was up a big white fir tree, a very difacult place to get a shot and I had to go to the foot of the tree and shoot straight up. I shot him through the body. The tree was standind on the bank of the creek when he fell out of the tree he fell in a deep pool of water in the creek and there was a large rock in the middle of the water and he climed on this rock. Old Watch would swim around and barking, and he got to close and the cougar reached out with one of his paws and caught him by the side of his head with his claws and was holding the dog and looking at me. He did not hold Watch long till I put a bullet between his eyes. I skined him and I think he measured about 8 feet and 9 1/2 and I think Alf Sawtelle measured him. The neighbors were glad I killed him for they were bad after sheep and hogs and calfs and colts, and are a dangerous animal to be in the woods. and I give him a hind quarter to take home with him. I was hunting on Coal Creek, for bear, that a man had traped two of his toes off. I could easily track him by the shape of foot. I followed on till he went into a big swamp. I sent the dogs around on one side and I went on the other and stoped and waited for the dogs to bring him out. A man by name of Whitlock took up a bunch of horses and they was feeding near this swamp. When they brought him out, it scared the horses and they run to me and was all around me, when the bear came I could not shoot, for fear of killing a horse. There was a ridge ahead of him that he aimed to cross near the top of this ridge was a log. A bear will always jump on a log when crossing it

and are a dangerous animal to be in the woods. and I give him a hind quarter to take home with him. I was hunting on Coal Creek, for bear, that a man had traped two of his toes off. I could easily track him by the shape of foot. I followed on till he went into a big swamp. I sent the dogs around on one side and I went on the other and stoped and waited for the dogs to bring him out. A man by name of Whitlock took up a bunch of horses and they was feeding near this swamp. When they brought him out, it scared the horses and they run to me and was all around me, when the bear came I could not shoot, for fear of killing a horse. There was a ridge ahead of him that he aimed to cross near the top of this ridge was a log. A bear will always jump on a log when crossing it

*   *   *

CHAPTER IX

Wilhoit Springs Resort

"Curative Mineral Water Discovered
in South Clackamas County" . . . . by Gail McCormick

Everybody who was "somebody" visited Wilhoit Springs Resort - and dressed up for the occasion. This photo is of the Milsters - Jet Dibble's family. ca. 1894. *Courtesy of Molalla Historical Society.*

Bibliography:
Author Unknown, "Historic Hotel Destroyed by Fire," *Molalla Pioneer*, February 24, 1916
Author Unknown, "Early Settlers Remembered," *The Bulletin*, January 15, 1975
Author Unknown, "Wilhoit Springs Appealed to Summer Campers," *The Bulletin*, June 13, 1979
Kohler, Vince, "Firm Sees Money Flowing from Spring," *Oregonian*, February 14, 1982
Lynch, Vera, "Recreational Facilities," *Free Land for Free Men*, 1973
Schmeiser, Carl, "Wilhoit Water Good for What Ails You," *The Bulletin*, December 19, 1973
Todd, Bob, "Oregon Water to be Bottled & Sold Nationwide," *Molalla Pioneer*, January 13, 1982

"*Curative Mineral Water Discovered in South Clackamas County*"

by Gail McCormick

One of the most renowned of the early parks in Clackamas County was Wilhoit Springs, named for John Wilhoit who took up a land claim in 1869 at the site. Located an hour's drive from Portland, in a grove of virgin firs in the beautiful wooded hills at the foot of the Cascade mountains, the park was a popular vacation spot from the 1890s on. There are two springs at Wilhoit, one pleasantly soda and the other highly sulphur. The soda spring was accidentally discovered by John Bagby, an avid hunter, when he tracked a deer to the spot in 1868. The mineral

properties of the water left a rich sediment around the spring that deer used as a salt lick.

Water Known Internationally

International fame came to Wilhoit in 1884 when Mr. T. Edward Herman, a well-known Catholic priest, visited the Springs to find relief from rheumatism. He derived such great benefit from the use of the water that he determined to send an analysis to a reliable German doctor of high standing. He believed European authority on such things

Wilhoit Mineral Springs

MOLALLA
Oregon. Route 1

Open all year

C. A. CLARK, Mgr.
Phone 60-F-2, Molalla

good roads!

Scenery

Picnicing

Fishing

Camp fires

Horses

Baths

Dining Service

Dancing

Store

The lure of Wilhoit Springs Resort is depicted in this ca. 1930 advertising brochure: the virgin forest, the

to be far more trustworthy than any other. The result of his action was set forth in a prominent, illustrated German paper, "Deutsche Hausohatz," between the summers of 1884 and 1885:   "The Wilhoit Springs mineral waters, judging from the remitted analysis, belongs to that species of springs - and even to the most efficient of that class - which contain iron, common salt and carbonic acid. Their composition is very near the same as that of the famous

Ragoozi and Tandar Springs at Kissengen, and correspond, consequently, with the same salutary effects. They can be used internally and externally.   The best results will be obtained in chronic diseases of the exterior skin, of the mucous membrane, and of the organs of respiration in disturbances of digestion, nervous complaints, rheumatism, gout, scrofula, swelling of the milt, fever, piles and obesity."   Thus the Springs

cute little peaked roof huts, the spacious log lodge, the restful atmosphere and curative soda water.

established a place in the international scientific world as among the most efficient in their class.

The late Al Schoenborn, owner of the resort in the 1950s said: "The water has a lot of different and supposedly beneficial minerals, and for some a little hard to get used to at first, but it's generally enjoyed by a lot of us. It's good for what ails you."

In the early years, people would dip the water out of the spring and later a small pitcher pump was installed. For a long time a nominal charge was made to those who wished to carry the water away.

**Favorite Playground of
Clackamas County Elite**
In 1873, a frame hotel and dance hall were constructed

and a big Fourth of July celebration was held at Wilhoit. In 1880, Wilhoit sold twenty two and one-half acres of the forested property to Frank McLaren. He could see the value of having a resort built around the springs and he "slashed out a road" toward Molalla, and applied for a post office. An office was awarded in 1882, called Wilhoit. More improvements were made including unusual little peaked-roof cottages that rented for $1.50, $2 or $3 a week. The hotel was $2 per day or $10 to $12 per week. For camping privileges, 50 cents per week for each adult person; baths, each 25 cents, mud baths, each $2.50. A dance hall and bowling alley were built along with a memorable, octagonal bandstand and Wilhoit Springs was ready for business.

The resort was advertised as "an attractive spot, located near the mountains giving it an invigorating atmosphere, and surrounded with everything calculated to bring rest and rejuvenation to the weary and suffering."

In an age when medical assistance was at a minimum, the claim was made that the water could be used in many ways from a nasal "snuff" to a vaginal douche and would cure a variety of physical ailments from typhoid fever to female problems. For rheumatism "visit the Springs where you can drink and bathe freely. Rheumatism from uric acid in the blood is greatly relieved by drinking the water freely." As a nasal catarrh "snuff the water, lukewarm, up the nose, one nostril at a time. A nasal syringe or douche three times a day is better." And as a boon for suffering women "water containing Wilhoit Mineral Salts is unsurpassed as a vaginal injection for the relief and cure of female complaints." And of course, it was good for tummy aches, kidney and liver complaints, etc.

Everybody who was "somebody" went to Wilhoit in the early 1900s. The dinners at the hotel were famous and elaborate. And - the entertainment was equal to any found in the city. The circular, peaked-roof bandstand provided a proper stage for the fiddlers, horns and drums creating the music for couples to dance to on a large expanse of green lawn.

Travel to Wilhoit
an Adventure

Most say travel to Wilhoit, in the early days, was part of the pleasure of the vacation. Link Waldron and his nephew Clyde Waldron operated a stage line to Molalla until the Willamette Valley Southern Trolley was built in 1913. In the winter, when the roads were too difficult for automobile travel, horses were used. Traveling from Mt. Angel, a daily stage ran to Wilhoit and from Oregon City, two automobiles ran daily. Mr. McLaren's automobiles

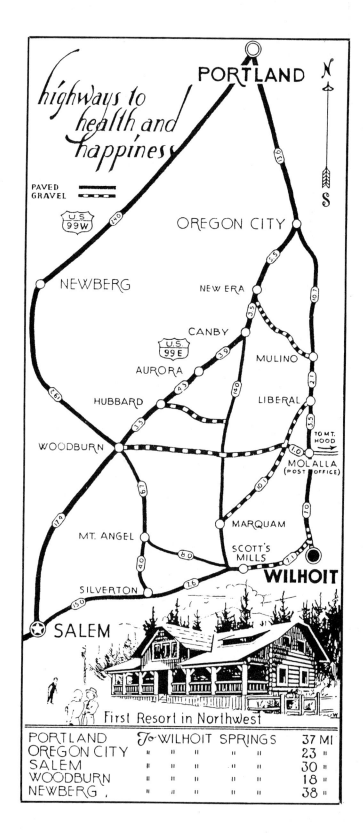

highways to health and happiness

PAVED
GRAVEL

PORTLAND

N
S

OREGON CITY

NEWBERG

NEW ERA

CANBY

MULINO

AURORA

LIBERAL

HUBBARD

TO MT. HOOD

WOODBURN

MOLALLA
(POST OFFICE)

MT. ANGEL

MARQUAM

SCOTT'S MILLS

SILVERTON

WILHOIT

SALEM

First Resort in Northwest

PORTLAND	To WILHOIT SPRINGS	37 MI
OREGON CITY	" " " " "	23 "
SALEM	" " " " "	30 "
WOODBURN	" " " " "	18 "
NEWBERG	" " " " "	38 "

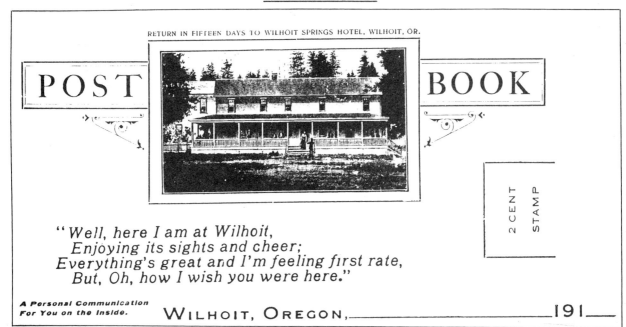

RETURN IN FIFTEEN DAYS TO WILHOIT SPRINGS HOTEL, WILHOIT, OR.

POST BOOK

2 CENT STAMP

"*Well, here I am at Wilhoit,
Enjoying its sights and cheer;
Everything's great and I'm feeling first rate,
But, Oh, how I wish you were here.*"

**A Personal Communication
For You on the Inside.**   WILHOIT, OREGON,_____191__

A ca. 1915 post book shows the original lodge that burned in 1916 and the early stage from Mt. Angel that transported the visitors. A daily stage ran from Mt. Angel and Mr. McLaren, the man who first seriously promoted Wilhoit Springs purchased two large, nine-passenger McIntyre cars, 1910 model, one seven-passenger Haynes car, one five-passenger Kissel-Kar, and one large McIntyre baggage car for transportation from Oregon City over unimproved and plank roads.

became a prominent feature of the resort. He had purchased two large, nine-passenger McIntyre cars, 1910 model, one seven-passenger Haynes car, one five-passenger Kissel-Kar, and one large McIntyre baggage car, to guarantee the best of transportation over the roads that were sometimes made of plank but, more often, dirt

and mud.

What was an adventure for some was a hardship for others. The late Dr. L. L. Pickins, Oregon City dentist and captain of Company I, Second Oregon Cavalry, told how his men were conditioned to endure the heat of the Philippines before shipping out during the Spanish

One imagines that Wilhoit Springs was "the place" for young people to meet a future husband or wife. This group of young adults is from upper left: W. P. Dibble, Charley Levitte, Frank Spore, Ona Austin, Minnie Austin, Etta E. Adams, Mattie Levitte, Lidy Austin and Effie B. Adams. ca. 1894. *Photo courtesy of Molalla Historical Society.*

American War. They were ordered to march in full battle regalia from Oregon City to Wilhoit on a hot summer day. If the farmers' wives and daughters along the twenty one mile route had not brought out cool drinks, they might not have survived.

Time Takes Its Toll

Time and nature have taken their toll on Wilhoit Springs. The first frame hotel burned in 1916 and the second log hotel, along with other buildings, burned in 1920. Two years later McLaren passed away. The bath house, where the huge stove heated water for the baths, fell into ruin. The large building over the pump is gone and all that is left is a large tile on end over the spring. Al and Mae Schoenborn revived the grounds for about ten years in the 1950s. And then the Columbus Day Storm took its toll on

what was left at the park. After the Schoenborns, the property changed hands a couple of times and is now owned by Clackamas County Department of Parks. In 1982, a company from Salem, Oregon, named Tracel started a project to bottle and sell the water. They say the water was excellent but lost their financial backing and could not continue with the project.

Wilhoit's Future

Diana Jensen, Operating Supervisor of Parks for Clackamas County, says a study will begin in 1992 regarding partial historic restoration and reconstruction of Wilhoit Springs as part of an on-going project to improve parks in the Molalla area. The Wilhoit project is scheduled for fiscal year 1993-1994.

*   *   *

CHAPTER X

The Dibbles of Molalla

"Carpenter Given 320 Acres to Build Home" .... by Gail McCormick

The Dibble House on South Molalla Avenue is owned and cared for by the Molalla Historical Society. Here society member, Frank Williams, pauses for a rest from his work on a new brick sidewalk. The tree to the right of the house is one of the apple trees planted by Horace Dibble. *Photo from the author's collection.*

Bibliography:
Bledsoe, Gloria, "Dibble House a Historical Treasure," Capital Journal, October 27, 1970
Chelson, Douglas, "History of the Families Buried in Austin-Dibble-Jackson-Larkins Cemetery," November 30, 1979
Published Manuscript
Garley, Neta of Portland, Oregon, Unrecorded Interview, August, 1991
Hardy, Marie, "The Dibble House Story", Published Manuscript, June 26, 1975

"Carpenter Given 320 Acres to Build Home"

by Gail McCormick

The year was 1854 - land was cheap and a good carpenter was hard to find. So Horace Dibble offered 320 acres of land to a former sea captain turned carpenter and a salt box style home, common in New England but rarely seen in Oregon, was built near the Four Corners of Molalla.

The house was finished in 1857 and this same house has been lovingly cared for by the Molalla Historical Society since 1969. Built of fir and cedar, the house is sturdy and well-constructed, containing more windows than the average pioneer dwelling. The fir floors were placed using square nails and the thresholds in the home are several inches lower than the floors because of the many footsteps that have crossed over them through the years.

Dibble House Warm & Cozy

A special feature of the home is a cozy little bedroom-sitting room just off the kitchen. You can easily envisage Julia Dibble rocking a baby there as the room contains a small brick fireplace, one of two of the house's fireplaces. The house was originally heated only by these two fireplaces and the kitchen wood stove. The two downstairs bedrooms contain rope spring beds topped with fancy hand-pieced quilts.

The kitchen is furnished with a long table and eight chairs from the Aurora Colony period. A wood cook stove, an enormous pie safe and the usual dry sink used by housewives of that day accompany the calico-covered table.

A narrow stairwell, lined with cedar, leads to the upstairs where Julia Dibble kept the loom on which she made rag carpets that were sold to neighbors.

Indians Loved Apples

Another famous feature of this historical home are the apple trees that Horace and Julia Dibble carefully planted and nourished in the mid 1800s. As the small orchard matured and ripened, settlers and Indians alike came from miles around to purchase apples from the Dibble's abundant trees. Three of these trees are still proudly standing near the Dibble House. The late Ina Dibble

Horace and Julia Ann Sturges Dibble
*1815 - 1899 * 1825 - 1904*
ca. 1860
Photo courtesy of Neta Garley.

remembered well the delicious apples that grew in the large orchard and were stored on shelves in the cellar and how the Molalla Indians used to come from across the river to buy apples from her grandparents. One incident she related was when Beaver Trapper and some of the squaws came in the spring and asked for apples. Horace Dibble told them there were apples down in the cellar but they were all soft and spoiled, however, they could have any that they wanted. Evidently the Indians idea of a good apple wasn't the same as the settlers for they started munching away with gusto, and even filled several

Thomas and Marian Long Dibble. ca. 1880.
Photo courtesy of Neta Garley.

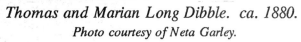

Ina and Guy Dibble,
the children of Tom and Marian Dibble. ca. 1900.
Photos courtesy of the Molalla Historical Society.

gunnysacks with apples and carried them away - as happy as could be.

Apple Festival Originated

In 1975 the Molalla Historical Society decided to initiate a yearly celebration of the apple harvest. The popular Apple Festival is held every year the second weekend in October. Plenty of freshly pressed apple cider and home made apple pie, donated by the Molalla community's expert pie makers and topped with ice cream, is available to tantalize taste buds.

Also on hand are pioneer era crafters with demonstrations of a time of self-sufficiency. In the Dibble's day, food was home-preserved, blankets were hand-woven and clothes were spun. One can see how old timers pressed apple cider and hand churned butter. There are demonstrations of spinning, weaving, candle making, soap making and bead making. Music is provided by old-time entertainers.

After making the hard overland journey over the Oregon Trail in 1852 with their first three children, Horace and Julia Dibble settled on a 640 acre donation land claim in the Needy area. Eliza Emily was six years old, Fayette was four and Roswell little more than a year. The overland journey was very difficult for the family. During the trip, Eliza was bitten on the leg by a rattlesnake and

The Dibble daughters and their husbands, from left: Eliza Emily and A. J. Sawtell, Myra Sylvinia and William H. Lewis, Annie Florinda and John K. Wilson. ca. 1880. Photo courtesy of Molalla Historical Society.

The property, a section of 640 acres, belonged to a widow Rachel Larkins. He purchased the land and arranged with the carpenter to build the type of house his ancestors had lived in - a "salt box."

The Dibble Children

By 1868 the Dibble family had grown to eight children: Eliza Emily (b. 1846, m. Alfred Sawtell), Fayette (b. 1848, never married), Roswell T. (b. 1851, m. Jett L. Milster), Thomas Leroy (b. 1854, m. Marian Long), Myra Sylvinia (b. 1856, m. William H. Lewis and Arthur Kayler), Jesse Morton (b. 1859, d. 1863), Annie Florinda (b. 1861, m. John K. Wilson), and Walter Perry (b. 1868).

The firstborn, Eliza Emily, became an expert seamstress. She married Alfred Sawtell in 1869 and they had one child, Iva May.

The second child, Fayette, died at twenty years of age.

Roswell T. Dibble, known as Rod, married Jett Milster from Silverton in 1877. They lived in the Dibble House with Rod's parents and had one daughter, Ola. Rod was an epileptic and had frequent seizures. He belonged to the Molalla Grange and caused considerable excitement during some of the Grange rituals when a seizure would occur. Apparently Jett believed epilepsy to be inherited so when Ola met Cal Warrick and they wanted to marry, Jett prevented them from living together until Ola was past the child bearing age. Finally they did live together, built a large house on Warrick road and traveled extensively.

Thomas Dibble bought land near Russellville in 1908, paying $1,000 for 220 acres at a sheriff's sale. He married Marian Long in 1897 and they also lived in the Dibble House until they had purchased land. In 1912 they built

that leg never grew properly. She was always to have a bad leg that prevented her from running about normally. Horace was ill much of the trip and never fully regained his health. One day, while living at Needy, Horace rode out looking for some lost cattle. His quest took him south of the Four Corners of Molalla to a little knoll that he immediately fell in love with and wanted for a home site.

Walter Dibble. ca. 1890.
Photo courtesy of Mildred Harless.

Roswell T. (Rod) and Jett L. Milster Dibble
with their daughter Ola. ca. 1900.
Photo courtesy of Neta Garley.

a homestead-style frame house. Tom worked at farming, logging and at one time worked a clay mine on their property. Tom and Marian had two children: Guy and Ina. The Dibbles were well known locally as a very musical family. They played fiddles and Ina played the dulcimer. The Dibble Orchestra played for many local celebrations and dances. Guy married Mary Mulvihill in 1915 and they were childless. Guy had an interesting business selling medicine and mineral powder. Ina never married and lived to be the last of her family in the Molalla area. She had one sweetheart who was killed in World War I. He presented her with a gift of a small twig table with a heart design which is on display in the Dibble House in Molalla. Many articles have been written about Ina, who lived alone but claimed she was never lonely. She believed in hard work and a simple life. Her needs were simple and her special love was music. She often played her dulcimer for those who would listen.

Myra (Maria) had two marriages, William H. Lewis and Arthur Kayler. By her first marriage she had two sons, Rex W. and Mark T. Lewis. Her second marriage to Arthur Kayler lasted only four years, ending when she accidently drowned in 1902.

Annie (Amy) married John K. Wilson and they moved from the Molalla area.

Walter lived with his mother until her death. He then left the Molalla area and no one seems to know what happened to him.

*   *   *

CHAPTER XI

Molalla's Early Celebrations

Nina Dunton was Miss Molalla in 1913 for the celebration of the arrival of the first train. She later became Mrs. Bob Elkins. *Photo courtesy of Mildred Harless.*

Bibliography:
*Author Unknown, "Molalla and Buckeroo Grew Up Together," Oregon City Enterprise, August 20, 1936
Jones, Beryl, "First Train Puffed Into Molalla in 1913," Published Manuscript, 1946*

PART ONE:

"First Train Puffed Into Molalla in 1913"

by Beryl Jones

"Back in 1913, when 25 miles was a considerable distance between cities, and a trip to Portland in a "machine" was quite an event, Molalla took the spotlight September 19, when her first train came puffing into town, heralded by a crowd of racing cowgirls, and witnessed by a crowd of 5,1000 persons from Portland, Oregon City and neighboring districts.

"Business men of the town turned out in full force, a big tent was erected for the speeches that go with such a celebration, and one of the attractive young ladies of the town was chosen to be the Goddess of Liberty and held aloft her torch during the procession of celebrities, railroad dignitaries and visiting nabobs.   At the time of her triumph over other young ladies of the town she was Miss

Nina Dunton, and was gowned in white, with a ribbon lettered with "Molalla" across her bosom.

"Everybody attended the big celebration and assisted in placing Molalla on the official railroad map. The track was 10.2 miles long, from Canby to Molalla, and was laid by the Portland, Eugene and Eastern Railway company in 1912-13, to be acquired later, July 1, 1915, by the Southern Pacific company.

"From the time the train poked its nose into the city about 10:30 a. m., until the last auto whirled away late in the evening it was a gala day that was long remembered in Clackamas County.

"From the files of the Oregon City Courier, issue of September 25, comes the report that "true to the promises

The arrival of the first train in Molalla, September 19, 1913, prompted a gun-toting, hooting and hollering, dress-up celebration complete with parade. The people in this photo of the "old bank building" in Molalla are unidentified. Today the building still stands at the interrsection of Main Street and South Molalla Avenue. *Photo courtesy of Molalla Historical Society.*

made by President Strahorn, of the new line, the PE andE branch line was ready for business on scheduled time, and three monster trains, doubleheaders and about ten coaches in each, made the maiden trip over the newly-ballasted roadbed."

"It was a day of thrills for the Molalla folk, but the biggest thrill of all, according to the record, was when the smoke from the first train, the Portland-Oregon City special, was seen in the distance. In true frontier style the incoming excursion was escorted into town by a bevy of cowgirls. Charlie Albright, of Albright and Holman Garage, Molalla, remembers that Frank Gray was the engineer for the special train.

"A parade was formed at the spot where the depot was later erected, and cowgirls, Indians, railroad officials, bands, rigs, autoists and excursionists marched to the big tent pitched near the fair grounds where the exercises of the day were held.

"Two features of the big parade were "Old Buck," the buckskin stage horse who had traveled more than 70,000 miles between Oregon City and Molalla, and Indian Henry, the last of the Molalla Indians, a sturdy old Indian who had been a fixture of the country for the past 67 years. These two were given places of honor in the parade.

"The coming of the railroad meant a well-earned rest for Old Buck. As for Henry, reports have it that, although in full regalia, he took things stoically and refused to comment on the proceedings of the day, which seemed rather to bewilder than to enthuse him.

"Under the big tent the oratory flowed like molasses in July. The speakers were many, and all were fluent in their congratulations to the people of the section on their new railroad. Among those who spoke were Robert E. Strahorn, president of the new line: Edgar E. Piper, president of the Portland Commercial Club: Mr. Pierce, Portland: Mr. D'Arcy, Salem, and Judge Grant Dimmick, Oregon City. The exercises at the tent were conducted by G. S. Taylor, editor of the Molalla Pioneer.

"President Strahorn was the first speaker, and modestly refused to take any credit for the completion of the new line, although it was instrumental in not only the preliminary work but in the actual construction and hasty completion of the new roadbed. In his speech Strahorn informed the audience that it was a day of double celebration for him, for it also was his 16th wedding anniversary.

"Edgar Piper, editor of the Oregonian, made, the Courier files state; a rattling good talk in his usual witty and delightful manner, and his talk, too, was along the lines of general rejoicing." He pointed out the cooperation of the Portland Commercial Club, and urged greater activity among the Molalla boosters.

"After the meeting in the tent had come to a close the crowds surged about the fairgrounds. The Molalla fair was in progress, and for the thousands in the town for the celebration it was a real carnival.

"About 2 p. m. the cowgirls, in real life "some of Molalla's fairest daughters," held a series of exciting horse races, followed by bronco busting. The report in the Courier says "the ponies all were mastered without any leather pulling, and fortunately for the large crowd which surged across the field and which the officials were unable to keep behind the fences, the horses bucked just enough to lend excitement to the afternoon and not enough to be really dangerous to the crowd."

"There was a ball game, too, and a long list of attractions that one would expect on such an occasion as the opening of a new railroad.

"The new line proved a great thing for the Molalla country. It skirted the rich Liberal country and the fertile region between Canby and Molalla. A train service was established at once, and during the Canby fair week, which followed the railroad opening and Molalla fair, the new line ran double train service between the two towns.

"Molalla did itself proud in handling the huge crowd, estimated at about 5,000. Three special trains went from Portland, Salem and Woodburn. About 200 Oregon City people took the Portland special as it went through town, and many local people went by automobile. The Courier states that "although eating facilities were at a premium, owing to the monster crowd, the Courier didn't hear of anyone going hungry.

"The big celebration had one sad aftermath. Tuesday morning, after the big day, Harry Clark, an Indian, came into Molalla and told authorities that Molalla Indian Henry, who had occupied such a prominent place in the day's festivities, had taken sick and died. A searching party went after the body, which they found on the roadside near Molalla. Slight bruises about the head and arms indicated that the old Indian had fallen from his buggy, or that foul play had been done.

"Sheriff Mass of Oregon City, on the theory that the famous old character might have been murdered, hurried to Molalla, where Clark, who was known as a "bad Indian," was taken into custody.

"Reports were brought in that old Henry, who was well past 70, had kept right on celebrating after the big day in Molalla, and had been on a "binge" at Mt. Angel. After Clark had steadfastly denied any knowledge of how Henry died, and authorities had been unable to pin anything on him, they reached the conclusion that Henry had imbued too much firewater, and had fallen from the buggy and died from the effects of the fall and liquor.

"Henry was the best known Indian in Clackamas County

and possessed white friends by the hundreds. He had lived on his homestead some distance from Molalla the last eight or 10 years of his life, and had lived in the Molalla country all his life. He had one son, Fred, who at the time was a logger in Washington. The Molalla people gave the old man a Christian burial.

"In another column on the front page of the Courier of September 25 is a list of the new Molalla city officers. The town was incorporated a short time before the advent of the railroad, and W. W. Everhart was elected mayor without any opposition. Councilmen were W. D. Echerd, Fred M. Henriksen, William Mackrell, L. W. Robbins, A. T. Shoemake and I. M. Tolliver, D. C. Boyles was chosen recorder and Fred Havemann treasurer. Fred R. Coleman was elected marshall. The report gives us the information that "the vote was not a large one for the town, and comparatively few of the women took any interest whatsoever in the election."

*   *   *

In the afternoon the cowgirls, in real life "some of Molalla's fairest daughters" held a series of exciting horse races.

A crowd of 5,000 witnessed the arrival of the "first train".

SCENES
FIRST TRAIN TO ARRIVE
MOLALLA
OPENING
P.E. & E. RY'S Sept 19 1913
AUSPICES
PORTLAND COMMERCIAL CLUB

Jack Vernon and "Old Buck", the stage horse. ca. 1913.
Photo courtesy of Molalla Historical Society.

Early Molalla Volunteer Fire Department. The fire department took over the Buckeroo to raise money for the department. Only identified is Harry Harvey, the driver. ca. 1926. *Photo courtesy of Molalla Historical Society.*

PART TWO:

"Molalla & Buckeroo Grew Up Together"

Enterprise Courier — 8-20-1936

"In the early days as settlers began to find their way into the Molalla valley, two pioneer trails -- one running east and west and the other north and south -- were formed. It followed as a natural course that a town should grow up at the place where these two trails intersected. This spot is Molalla's well-known Four Corners, around which early stores and houses grouped themselves.

"Molalla, now as then, is the center for a large farming and lumbering district that extends far into the Cascade Mountains in the south and east. The history of Molalla is so intimately bound up with the people and resources of the surrounding countryside that the town seems to extend miles beyond its city limits. The families who first set up farms in this valley were for the most part those who later started businesses.

"The story of the Molalla country logically falls in three divisions. The first concerns the Indians.

"Sometime during the eighteenth century, the Molalla valley became the home of a group of Indians that had seceded from the Cayuses. The name "Molalla" that they took means grass country. These Indians were great hunters and delved deep into the Cascades. They were also brave warriors, but after suffering a terrific defeat at the hands of the Cayuses, they never again went out to battle.

"The first chief known to the white men here was named

The first Fourth of July celebration in Molalla was held July 4, 1911. *Photo courtesy of Gena Cline.*

Early Molalla Music Store float in the July 4, 1914 parade. J. V. Harless team with Martin Boyles, J. V. Harless and Fenton Harless in the front seat. *Photo courtesy of Mildred Harless.*

Klooster. However, the Indian chief who is well-remembered yet today was Henry Yelkes (Indian Henry) who was killed in 1913. His murderer remains unknown. His second wife was Indian Nell, Beaver Trapper's daughter. She also met a violent death. Indian Henry was survived by a son, Fred Yelkes, who lived in Portland and was known as the last of the Molallas. In 1845 there were about 150 Indians here.

"After the white men came, a reservation was laid out for the Molallas. Blazed trees marked the limits of the reservation. One of these trees still stands on the John Vick place. Another tree was on the Ridings' place and another stood near the present Bowlin place. The Indians made their headquarters in the Dickey Prairie country.

"With the coming of white men, the valley entered into the second period of its development. Rev. Jason Lee is said to have followed up the Molalla River on his way to Salem in 1837. However, the first white man really to come into the valley was William Russell, who came here in 1840 and found no one but Indians. In 1845, William Barlow settled on what is now the Faurie place. He later sold his 640 acres for $2000 in wampum and cattle. This land took in territory covered by many prosperous farms.

"In 1843, William H. Vaughan brought the first wagon to Molalla. The next few years brought many well-known Molalla families here. John Trullinger was the first white person to be born here.

"In 1853, the Preston Barger family came through Molalla. There were still no stores and the country was sparsely settled. The Bargers forded the Molalla at the steel bridge and entered the valley along that trail.

"Augustus Engle established the first store in Molalla in 1857. Andrew J. Stubbs was the second storekeeper and the first postmaster. He was also an early teacher here. Dr. Welch was the first dentist and Dr. Sanford was the first doctor.

"It was during this period that much of the lore grew up about the Molalla country that newcomers here find so interesting and unusual. This Molalla tradition may be explained by the fact that Molalla previously was a valley off to itself at the base of unexplored mountains. Large family groups became established here, intermarried and worked together in exploring the resources and building up the country. These families still have many reminiscences to share about the first schools, who planted various trees and who drank the first Wilhoit water. Their interest and the interest of their descendants in the entire district is deeply rooted. New residents often

Early Molalla Buckeroo directors: Top row from left: Sid Powers (postmaster), Mort Cochrell, Walter Taylor, Bob Masterston and Bill Miller. Bottom row from left: Fred Parks, Duane Robbins (banker), Art Farr, Henry Dahl and Jim Riddell (grocer). *Photo courtesy of Molalla Historical Society.*

remark that there is "something about the town that gets you".

"It was also during this period that Molalla gained a reputation of being one of the liveliest spots in the country. The often-quoted statement that there was a saloon on every corner is a gross exaggeration, but plenty of hard liquor was drunk. Pioneer mothers have been heard to tell how drunks would gallop up and down the roads on their horses, occasionally firing random shots. Indians also would gallop at full speed up to the houses, and the mothers were kept in constant worry for the safety of their children coming home from school. One saloon keeper shot a man in the back who had been doing some unliked gossiping. Some of the store buildings had bullet holes in them.

"In the year 1913 Molalla started out on its third period of development. September 19 of that year saw the first

Southern Pacific train pull into Molalla. A big celebration marked the event. To add to the excitement of the afternoon's program, someone thought it would be interesting to bulldog a few steers and ride some local bucking horse. Thus was born the idea that ten years later resulted in the Molalla Buckeroo.

"And with the boon that followed the coming of the railroad, Molalla became a 'city'. W. W. Everhart, now county treasurer, took the oath of office as Molalla's first mayor October 4, 1913. On that first council were L. W. Robbins, W. T. Echerd, I. M. Toliver, A. T. Shoemake, W. M. Mackrell and Fred M. Henriksen. The last named had lived in Molalla only five months at the time. D. C. Boyles was the first recorder; F. G. Havemann, the treasurer, and Fred R. Coleman, the marshall.

"Other Molalla mayors in the order that they were elected have been Fred Henriksen, Ralph Holman, W. T. Echerd,

Molalla Buckeroo Queens

1918 — Glades Baite (Bony)

1925 — Anita Cole (Powers)

1926-1935 — information not available

1936 — Geraldine Fergison (Brown)

1937 — LaVanda Bunke (Nicole)

1938 — Aleena Cutting (Hendrickson)

1939 — MaryAnn Hill (Lawton)

1940 — Anna Mae Dunrud (Cutting)

1941 — Lois Thronson (Lay)

1942 — not available

1943 — not available

1944 — Helen Warren (Wagner)

1945 — Joan Tanner (Youngren)

1946 — Marilyn Buxton (Landeen)

1947 — Ellen Johnson (Thronson)

1948 — Delores Long (Peterkin)

1949 — Kathryn Erickson (Snyder)

1950 — Louise Miller

1951 — Beverly Owens (Chaney)

1952 — Donneva Sheppard (Aschoff)

1953 — Lorraine Ridenour

1954 — Marilyn Sawtell (Behrends)

1955 — Helen Miller (Barklow)

1956 — Barbara DuPont (Giddings)

1957 — Joan Newland (Clark)

1958 — Judy Kappler (Strader)

1959 — Anna Marie Rau

1960 — ZoAnn Lindas Lewin

1961 — Barbara Day (Schlitt)

1962 — Joyce Kappler

1963 — Joan Toppi (Zuber)

1964 — Sue Myers (Keller)

1965 — Kathy Magill (Zeek)

1966 — Barbara Martin

1967 — Joan Watson (Jeskey)

1968 — Glenda Stewart (Franich)

1969 — Kathy Krammer

1970 — Debbie Patterson (Jensen)

1971 — Trudy Nielson

1972 — Kathy Weick

1973 — Sue Martin

1974 — Marta Todd (Lowry)

1975 — Judy Ruddel (Herndon)

1976 — Carolyn May (Postlewait)

1977 — Karen Whalen (Letcher)

1978 — Joni Harms (Wichman)

1979 — Sharron Rose (Kalmbach)

1980 — Barbara Best

1981 — Bonnie Block (Lewis)

1982 — Jodi Miller

1983 — Judy White (Taylor)

1984 — Brenda Bennett

1985 — Shelley Farlow

1986 — Marilyn Kosel

1987 — Jerilee Cooley (David)

1988 — DeeAnn Schlitt

1989 — Lisa Peterkin

1990 — Sara Lile

1991 — Victoria Holleman

1992 — Krista Ehrler

H. N. Everhart and the present mayor, W. J. Avison.

"The Molalla Pioneer, a weekly newspaper was first printed March 7, 1913. An electric light system was established in 1915. A telephone system has been in use since 1903. In 1917 the first street in Molalla was paved, and Molalla won much praise for having paved streets before other towns many times its size could boast them. Concrete sidewalks soon lined the streets. Molalla's first water supply came from a large well, but in 1921 a new water system was laid. The water supply comes from Trout Creek, a mountain stream eight miles east of Molalla.

"Another important event of the year 1913 was the beginning of the construction of a new school building. Molalla schools date back to 1856, and although the first of them were located east of Molalla, for many years the schools have been situated on the present grade school site. What was for that time a modern and well equipped building was ready for school in the fall of 1914. It housed both the high school and the grade school.

"Molalla abounds in community organizations, and they have gone ahead progressively in improving the town. A volunteer fire department has existed here for many years, but in 1925 the business men organized a new department that has added to Molalla's firefighting equipment through proceeds from the Buckeroo, dances and other undertakings.

"The first church was established here in 1870.

"The Molalla Women's Civic club paid for the site of the city park and finances its upkeep.

"A strong grade school Parent-Teacher association has undertaken as one of its principal projects the supplying of warm lunches to school children. The association has also gone ahead with extensive work in the improvement of health conditions among the children. It also sponsors a Camp Fire group, a Boy Scout troop and Four-H clubs.

Northwest corner of Main intersection - Molalla, Oregon. 1913. *Photo courtesy of Mildred Harless.*

South Molalla Avenue - Molalla, Oregon. 1913. *Photo courtesy of Mildred Harless.*

"A large membership is enjoyed by the Molalla Grange. The Grange owns its own two story building. Principal fraternal organizations are the Odd Fellows, Rebekahs, Masons and Eastern Stars. Business men have a Commercial Club that has sponsored free shows once a week during the past two summers. Two different railroads have come into Molalla, but they no longer operate passenger lines. Busses serve the community. Good highways lead out of Molalla in all direction. Molalla is 18 miles from Oregon City and 35 miles from Portland.

"The teasel ranch operated by George H. Gregory much interest among visitors. The teasel are used in eastern textile mills to raise the nap of fabrics. The cutting, growing and shipping of the teasel give employment to many persons.

"Lumbering is the principal industry of the section. Many small mills are operated near here. In 1924 the Eastern-Western company moved into the timbered section southeast of Molalla and set up nine camps. This brought many new families to Molalla. One of the largest stands of timber in the Northwest is owned by the Collins-Weyerhaeuser company east of Molalla. Small scale operations are being started this fall in this timber, and indications are that next spring extensive work will start.

"The building of summer homes along the creeks and rivers near Molalla is another development that is adding

First auto transportation from Oregon City to Molalla. Driver is L. Waldron with Oscar Miller and Mrs. Mayes in the back seat. Below photo shows the Molalla Grade School completed in 1914. *Both photos courtesy of Mildred Harless.*

Annie Stubbs Clifford.
Mrs. Clifford was in charge of the first telephone central in Molalla. She was the second postmistress of Molalla, appointed to her position in 1893. Her father, A. J. Stubbs, was Molalla's first postmaster, being appointed in 1874. The telephone system first came into use in the Molalla area in 1903. She was born in 1871 and was the second white child born in Molalla. ca. 1913. *Courtesy of Molalla Historical Society.*

to Molalla's business and growth. Many of these homes are of luxurious proportions. Molalla itself made a high national rating in a recent survey of its standard of homes.

"A fertile agriculture valley surrounds Molalla. Fruits, grains, flax may all be grown with ease.

"An outgrowth of Molalla's early "Celebrating" habits and of the small wild west show that was given in 1913 when the first train came in is the Molalla Buckeroo. The thirteenth annual Buckeroo was given last July 3, 4 and 5. Thousands of spectators viewed a successful performance. The Buckeroo has brought nation-wide publicity to Molalla.

"The first show in 1913 was so well received that each fall after that small shows were staged. Everett Wilson and Guy Ray were instrumental in putting on a number of these. One year the city council decided to sponsor the Round-Up, as it was then called. The city fathers could hardly believe their ears when they were told that the profits amounted to $1800. They had hoped to raise about $200 to buy the present Buckeroo grounds as a ball park for the city.

"The park was bought and the city decided to make the Round-Up an annual affair. Officers of the association were to be elected at a town meeting. The show was dropped for several years during the war, but is now an annual event."

* * *

The Molalla Pioneer

The original building was erected in 1874 on the southwest corner of Main and Molalla Avenues. The building was used as a typical country store until 1895 and later as a barber shop. The upper story served the public for social functions for many years. The front was battle-scarred, having been riddled by the bullets of horse thieves in a battle with citizens in Molalla's "wild and wooly" days. The building was torn down in the fall of 1913. A new Pioneer office was built in 1915. The first Molalla Pioneer, Molalla's weekly newspaper, was printed March 7, 1913. *Photo courtesy of Mildred Harless.*

CHAPTER XII

The Sawtells of Molalla

Bibliography:
Daugherty, Otis Ray, "Sawtell Family History", *Unpublished Manuscript*
Garley, Neta of Portland, Oregon, *Unrecorded Interview, August, 1991*
Gooding, Virginia Sawtell, "My Early Memories of Molalla", *Unpublished Manuscript*
Hines, Rev. H. K. DD, "A. J. Sawtell", <u>An Illustrated History of the State of Oregon</u>, *1893*
Kelly, M. A., "An Oregon Teasel Farm", <u>The Orange Judd Farmer</u>, *V. 26, #3, January 21, 1899*
Sawtell, Alfred Rolla, "Historical Data of Sawtell & Davis Families", *Unpublished Manuscript, 1954*

PART ONE:

"First Teasel on West Coast"

by M.A. Kelly

"A branch of agriculture but little known to most people, is the cultivation of teasels. Doubtless, many are aware that the teasel is used by manufacturers for raising the nap on woolen goods, but still they may have no definite idea of the plant, nor of its appearance while growing. It was my pleasure to visit the teasel farm of A. J. Sawtell, and to see the plant, itself, in its natural state. This farm, the only one of its kind in Oregon, is situated near Molalla, 32 miles southeast of Portland.

"The teasel plant, when well matured, averages nearly six feet in height, and resembles a thistle in appearance, having but little foliage, and being covered with half-blunt prickles, while the teasels correspond to the thistle heads or flowers. The color is a cool, silvery green, which turns grayer when dried. The perfect teasel is almost cylindrical in shape, but often in some queer freak a plant produces curiously deformed ones, some being double, while others assume a fan shape. They bloom first round the center, the fine, white flowers then tapering gradually to each end. When the seeds are ripe, the awns or tracts become stiff and prickly, and it is from these barbs that the teasel is considered valuable.

"The plants are set in rows the length of the field, far enough apart to allow the gatherer room to work

The teasel wagons, on the Sawtell farm, line up to haul teasel to the drying rooms. Pre 1900 photo.
Photo courtesy of Neta Garley.

conveniently. Each person wears buck skin gloves to protect his hands, and uses a short-handled knife, usually having a curved blade, to sever the teasel from the plant, he taking care to cut it with a three or four inch stem. On emptying his basket into the capacious wagon bed, which holds 120 bu, the cutter receives a check. Each basket contains 2 bu, and one pretty, brown-eyed little maid told me that she could fill 16 a day, while some could fill 19. She also added that each check was worth seven cents.

"From the field we returned to the house, and in company with Mr. Sawtell, who very courteously explained every detail, went through the dry house and trimming room. The dryer is a long narrow building 25 x 200 ft. The floors, eight in number, are composed of small, movable poles. Wagons are drawn up into the building by means of pulleys, and their contents spread over the top floor first. Then the poles of each succeeding floor are moved gently until the teasels have been sifted to the bottom. Four men are required in the work of unloading, one at each end and two at the side, to rake the teasels evenly over the floor. There were already 270,000 lbs of new teasels in this place, and the building was not filled. These, however, would weigh but a third as much when dry.

"On leaving this interesting building we went to the trimming house, where our guide kindly explained the cutting and the sorting process. The leaf-like projections round the base of the teasel are removed by hand, this part of the industry furnishing employment to a number of women and girls all winter. A machine, which also cut the stems in uniform length, was used formerly for trimming, but its work was not satisfactory. After the teasels are prepared, they are dropped through a gauge, which places each size by itself. The smallest measures one inch in circumference, and each succeeding size increases by a quarter of an inch until the maximum, three inches, is reached. The assorted teasels are stored in bins until required for shipment, when they are packed solidly in large boxes and sent to various points in the United States, for Mr. Sawtell not only furnishes the Pacific Coast market, but also supplies many of our eastern factories with teasels."

*   *   *

PART TWO:

"A. J. & Eliza Sawtell"

by Gail McCormick

Alfred Joseph Sawtell, pioneer teasel grower of the Pacific Coast, was born in England October 22, 1839.

A. J. and his sister, Mary, came to America in 1858. Having been educated in the teasel business in his native land, he and sister Mary carefully packed the family dishes in teasel seed when they left England hoping to be able to continue in this profession.

The first year of their arrival in America, the two siblings stayed in Canada. The next year they came direct to Clackamas County where A. J. purchased 310 acres of land a few miles north of the Four Corners of Molalla.

In 1860, A. J. Sawtell sowed the first teasel seed on the Pacific Coast, beginning on a small scale to see if he could produce a good article. He found satisfactory growth and began to increase his facilities for growing and processing teasel for market. An article in the 1893 "Illustrated History of the State of Oregon" referring to A. J. Sawtell states: "He has a large factory engaged in the preparation of the teasel for market. As his establishment is the only one in the West, and as his product is used extensively in the manufacture of all woolen goods requiring a nap, it finds a ready market on the coast. Mr. Sawtell thoroughly understands his business. He is the inventor of improved machinery for his work, and in his factory puts up eighteen grades of teasels."

In a brief, unpublished history about the early Molalla settlers, descendant Otis Ray Daugherty wrote: "At one time A. J. Sawtell employed about 30 Chinese in trimming the teasels. They operated machines of rotary, hollow, cylinder knives in which they would insert the stems. These knives cut so close to the burr that they would break off while being used in the woolen mills. This method was abandoned and the teasels were then trimmed by hand shears. The Chinese refused to do this so white labor was employed. The Chinese lived in a one room house east of Teasel Creek, where they cooked, slept, and sang songs. My brother, Fred, and I used to visit them; they would give us oranges, candy and fire

Alfred Joseph and Eliza Dibble Sawtell with daughter, Iva May. ca. 1890
Photo courtesy of Neta Garley.

crackers. When they would see us coming, they would say, "Here come Fleddy and Lay." They couldn't sound the letter R."

Just what is teasel, anyway? The word alone arouses one's curiosity. When one finds out the teasel was a peculiar, prickly, tuberous, cone shaped plant with springy hooks pointing back toward the stem, simply used for the raising of nap on material, it seems too great an effort just to have raised nap on material. However, dress was as important in those days as now. In the 17th Century,

Langland, in Piers Plowman, wrote:

"Cloth that cometh fro the weaving is naught comely to wear,

Till it is fulled under foot or in fulling stocks, Washen well with water, and with teasles scratched, Tucked and tented,

and under tailor's hand"

Fulling meant to soak, pound and press a fabric until it was shrunk and compact. Napping, raising the surface fibers or nap, was later done by wire brush. The sharp yet comparatively soft awns of the teasel had the advantage of being able to yield when a knot in the yarn was struck, preventing tearing, and producing lustrous, soft nap on broad cloth and a bright, clean weave on worsted suiting.

The history of the Sawtell family began with William Sawtell of Aller, Somersetshire, England, who married Lucy Coggan in 1818. This couple had seven children; George (b. 1819), John Newton (b. 1822 m. Lovena Loveridge), Henry Coggan (b. 1829 m. Nancy Jane Reed), William Oliver (b. 1831 m. Margaret Jane Todd), Mary Lock (b. 1836 m. James Lucien Ogle), Alfred Joseph and a son Frederick who died at the age of one year.

On May 14, 1848, the three older brothers, John Newton, Henry Coggan, and William Oliver, left the port of London, headed for America and landed at New York on June 12, 1848. In 1853, they, along with two wives and John and Lovena's baby daughter Mary, left Illinois and crossed the plains to Oregon to establish homesteads in Oregon near Molalla. John secured a donation land claim in September, 1853, southeast of Molalla and Henry Coggan secured his claim in December, 1854, near Reeces Butte (now known as Highland Butte). Later he bought a farm southeast of Molalla. Reportedly, William Oliver worked in the Salmon River gold mines, earning $900 to purchase 320 acres of a Hubbard donation land claim. There he settled down and married Margaret Jane Todd. George, the eldest son, remained in England but his son, Harry Sawtell, and his family came to America and lived near Molalla for some time. Sister Mary Lock married James Lucien Ogle and settled in the Rural Dell section, west of Molalla. All of the Sawtells listed in the census of 1860 are listed with the occupation of farmers.

The Sawtell Road southeast of Molalla is named for this family and Teasel Creek was named for the teasels grown there.

March 23, 1869, A. J. Sawtell married Eliza E. Dibble (b.

William Oliver & Margaret Jane Todd Sawtell
ca. 1880

1847), daughter of Horace Dibble, pioneer of 1852, thereby uniting two of the most prestigious families of the Molalla area. They had one daughter, Iva May (Lewis). A. J. & Eliza were charter members of the Molalla Grange. Mr. Sawtell was viewed by others as a man of integrity and excellent business qualifications. He harvested his last crop of teasel in 1899 and then the business was taken over by George H. Gregory.

A. J. passed away in 1901. Eliza Dibble Sawtell passed away in 1927. Both are buried in Adams Cemetery, southeast of Molalla.

*   *   *

CHAPTER XIII

The Robbins of Molalla

Dr. Ray Hall and Oliver Willard Robbins take a horse and buggy ride in Molalla. ca. 1910. *Photo courtesy of Molalla Historical Society.*

Bibliography:
Author Unknown, "Mrs Molalla Breezes In", Oregon Daily Journal, August 21, 1924
Cline, Gena of Molalla, Oregon, Unrecorded Interview, January, 1991
Hines, Rev. H. K. "Levi Robbins", An Illustrated History of the State of Oregon, 1893
Mittge, Kevin, "The Molalla Families", The Robbins & Herren Families of Pacific NW, 1988
Robbins, Harvey, "History of Jacob Robbins and Sarah Spillman", Published Manuscript, 1921

PART ONE:

"Oregon Trail Trek"

by Harvey Robbins

Written in 1921

Call of the West Strong

"The strain of adventure handed down to our Pappy, Jacob Robbins and others and the call of the West being strong, on March 19, 1852, we left our happy childhood home in Indiana and came to the unknown wilds of Oregon. Of this journey from Indiana to Oregon, I will now give you a brief sketch. We encountered many adventures and it took strong determination to meet some of the difficulties.

"We boys, on leaving Indiana, were big boys, myself, the eldest, being 18. My siblings were Levi, 16, Thomas, 15, Martin, 13, Oliver, 12, Nancy Jane, 10, Theodore, 8, Aaron, 5, and little Amanda Minerva, age 2. We boys wore our hair bobbed and were dressed in red cloth coats, long trousers, silk stove pipe hats and were blue eyed and rosy cheeked. All of the family was well-clothed for the journey by clothes made in the home and dyed by Aunt Polly Burke, one of Mother's sisters.

"Many relatives and friends were present to bid us farewell. Pappy planned to go to Oregon at the suggestion of Uncle Natty Robbins who sold his place the year before and had moved to Missouri. He returned to collect bills and settle up business with the intention of coming to Oregon Territory and wanted Pappy to come

"Pappy"
Jacob Robbins, Jr.
1809 - 1896

"Mother"
Sarah Robbins
1812 - 1865

with him. Pappy, deciding to make the trip, made a hasty sale of his farm and belongings not needed for the trip and got together necessary ox teams and equipment for the journey. Mother and helpers made woolen clothing and bedding. Some of the coverlets made then are still in the family. Having been in constant service, they still retain their beauty of design and coloring. The dyes being mostly Indigo blue, Madder, Cherry red and Walnut brown and were as lasting as the cloth. America was then in the making. Folks worked to complete a task not by the hour, there being no clocks, and got their reward from work well done.

"Uncle Natty was a doctor and his services were much in demand. William Robbins, his eldest son, came to Missouri one year before we left so their family joined the party near Huntsville. There were also six daughters in this family as follows: Amanda Minerva, Emiline (m. Absolom Barnes), Jan (M. John Hamilton), Mahala, Zobede (m. William Sharp), Nancy (m. Joseph Barstow), and Angeline. Amanda, Emiline and Mahala took cholera and died near "Dry Sandy", in what is now known as Kansas. All were buried in one grave. Six miles on at Little Blue River, Absolom Barnes died and was buried. This being the great cholera year, many were left by the wayside. Mother and Oliver of Pappy's family had it and Oliver was very bad but, they saved him by the use of good whiskey and strong pepper tea.

Stampedes Abundant On Trail

"When buying some oxen near Huntsville, the owner told me that I could ride one of them as it was broken and very gentle, so I climbed on. This one was next to the wheels of four yoke of oxen and some of these young oxen were not well broken so kept bucking around disturbing the leaders until they came to a long steep hill going faster and faster. I slid down my steeds back until I came to the yoke where I hung on for dear life until we reached the bottom of the hill and got going up the hill on the other side. The mud soon tired them out and I lived to tell the story. Pappy thinking that I would be killed got on the young mare and tried to overtake us but, Old Roan was not yet well broken so it only added to the excitement.

"In Missouri at the Little Platt River, we were across when two small families started across above the mill dam. One of their cows had a young calf and about midstream it took a notion to swim with the current, so over the dam it went and was washed ashore unharmed. The cows followed and went over but could never get out of the whirlpool below. As they were washed almost ashore the whirlpool would catch them and carry them under until they were exhausted and drowned. The young married

Levi & Harvey Robbins
ca. 1860
Photo courtesy of Molalla Historical Society

woman who owned the cows followed the shore and cried and called them by name, but all in vain, as they drowned. More than fifty years later, I was telling of this same tragedy to the gathering around the stove in Robbins Brothers Store at Molalla, when an old man called Uncle Peter Boyles spoke up saying that he could vouch for that as he was present at the time.

"One day the sun was shining bright on the plains when someone saw a glimmer far ahead and on coming nearer we investigated and found that it was a circle of real live skunks apparently having a war dance. They were standing on their front feet with their tails waving in the air and moving silently in a weird fashion. The glimmer was the sun shining on their fur.

"Pappy started with 21 yoke or big oxen from Missouri and six young mares. Only one of the mares, called Old Roan, withstood the journey. One of the mares was bitten by a rattle snake and an Indian man made them understand that it could be cured by burning around it with a hot iron if they would give him 'Heap big double hand-full of powder'. For evidence that they could cure a snake bite they showed a scar on one of their own ponies they had thus cured, but before Pappy had decided to let the Indians try the remedy, this nice young mare had died.

"We saw a buffalo stampede and also had our stock stampeded one evening by an army of beatles flying over us. The next stampede we had was this side of Little Blue River. Some of the young folks were riding and driving some of the loose stock, some of which had bells on, when they got way behind the train and thinking to catch up began cracking their whips and whooping and hurrying their own horses. The cattle got the spirit of the race and away they sped right into the train of 17 wagons. Levi drove the family wagon all the way, and he being the first to catch the warning yelled, Whoa Buck and Brandy" and they being prompt to obey set themselves so suddenly that the wheels run into them with such force that Levi, the most trusted and careful of Pappy's drivers, had to go over the top. Mr. John Hamilton, thinking he would help Levi reached back over his wagon and cracked his whip in their faces, at the same time losing control of his own team and away they all went in every direction, 17 covered wagons all heavily laden with four and five yoke of steers to each. One partnership wagon full of provisions and Mr. Hamilton's wagon wheels struck together with such force that all of the spokes were broken out of one wheel and they had to make a cart out of the wagon. Some of the wagons went up steep hills while others kept to the plains but all were going at full speed. One wagon turned over and Uncle Natty's daughter Zobede was under it until rescued. She is now 88 years old and remembers it all so vividly. One little girl said, as their wagon came to a halt, 'Mamma! Didn't we have a nice ride!'

"One incident was the killing of a fine big buck by some of the boys, which they could not bring into camp. They had started with the hams and it was getting late in the evening when they met a big grisly bear coming around the mountain side. It looked so fierce they dropped that nice venison and took the short cut for camp.

Pioneers Determined To
Reach Oregon

"At one stream some Mormon men had a ferry and charged five dollars for every wagon they took across. Pappy knew this was too much so started out and found a good place to cross and all got over safely so all other trains followed. Thus Mr. Mormon saw his dream of riches vanish and was in for revenge, so he planned and run off a lot of stock and fine horses which were never found. They made this appear to have been the work of Indians. However we got across without many Indian scares.

"At another crossing prices were too high to suit Pappy so he again jaunted to a place he believed all could get over safely saying, 'Block up boy'. The ferry man said, 'You can't do it.' One of the men replied, 'We're going to Oregon - you go to Hell!'

Wagon Party Breaks Up

"Uncle Natty and children settled about eight miles west of Oregon City near what is known as Tualatin. We left them at Old Fort Boise where they laid over for a more favorable wind for ferrying the river. Our family being short of food and very progressive decided to cross and come on.

"After leaving Uncle Natty, there were 23 in the party consisting of Jacob and Sarah Robbins, their seven sons and two daughters; myself, Levi, Thomas, Martin, Oliver, Jane, Theodore, Aaron and Amanda Minerva, who was only two years old at the time. Also, Miss Elizabeth Sharp, James Gardner, who drove one provision wagon and William French, who fell ill of lung fever near Fort Carney. I, then a lad of 18, drove the four yoke of oxen and nursed the sick man. Another man by the name of William Huff came on with them as one driver and another family by the name of Connor, man and wife, three sons, one daughter, one step son and one half brother. This made up the party until the supplies became so low that two of the men were sent on ahead to do as best they could for themselves.

Trek from The Dalles to
Barlows Hard & Tragic

"Levi drove the family wagon until we reached the Columbia Gorge at The Dalles. Pappy and Mr. Connor, with most of the big boys, drove the cattle down the river while the women and children and wagons were put on flatboats. At The Dalles we took the wheels off the wagons to make them as low as possible and loaded them with the provisions and families on two flatboats. We floated down the Columbia River until we reached the Cascades. It was snowing and raining and the two little boys were very ill. Here we unloaded the boats and portaged about four miles around the rapids on the north side of the river. The flat boats arrived at the Sandy River about two days before the stock. The stock was driven on the south side of the river until they reached a place opposite the mouth of the Sandy known as Parker's Landing. Here we had to swim the stock across again. Several of the men and boys including Tom, Martin, Levi and myself walked and drove the stock. It was cold and stormy, snowing and raining most of the time, making it hard on the travel worn band.

"Tom and I became ill of mountain fever and Tom had to ride most all of the way on the one horse. I was camp maker and it was my duty to go ahead and make camp

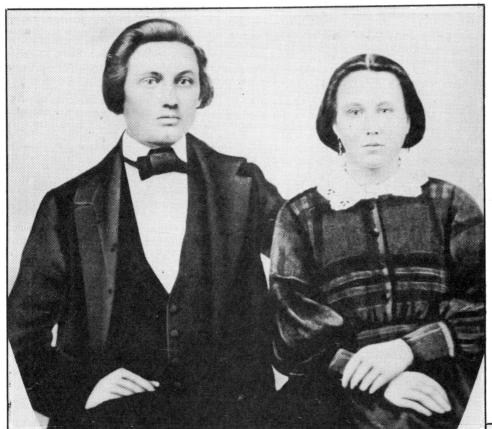

Levi and Ediff Barger Robbins. Top photo was taken from a postcard dated Christmas, 1910. The message on the post card read: "The original print was made in 1859 by Wiley Kenyon at Salem, Oregon. At that time we were aged 24 and 16 years. To Zella - from Grandpa and Grandma Robbins."

Levi and Ediff Barger Robbins in their elder years. From Salem Prairie most of the Robbins went to eastern Oregon. Jacob and Sarah Robbins and Levi and Ediff Barger Robbins came to the Molalla Prairie and purchased a large portion of the Swiegle Donation Land Claim just west of where Feyrer Park now stands. Levi and Ediff's children were: Oliver Willard (b. 1861, m. Annie Lilly), Lida Nettie (b. 1863, m. William P. Kayler), Ipha Pauline (b. 1865, never married), Sarah Martha (b. 1867, m. Philander J. Kayler), Mary Linnie (b. 1870, d. age 16), Della Gena (b.1873, m. William Arthur Shaver), Levi Wayne (b. 1876, m. Ione Rivers), and Everman (b.1881, m. Clara Bell Hayhurst). Many descendants of this large family still reside in the Molalla area. *Photos courtesy of Gena Cline.*

and cook meals. I was sick and rations were short so it was necessary to get camp meat whenever we could. On making camp at Castle Rock, I heard some Honkers (big geese) and noticing that one of them appeared to be tired, I got my rifle and shot its head off and had it for supper. We also killed several young grouse which helped supply the camp meat.

"Pappy came back and helped swim the stock across again at Sandy River. Then the men and boys, nine in number, got into a small row boat and were paddled across by Joe Connor. The boat was almost dipping water but the river was calm that evening and we were very quiet, so got safely over. By this time I was a very sick boy and death was in the camp and my little brother, Aaron, age 3, died that night.

"Mr. William Herrin came to our rescue at this camp, he having crossed in 1845 and settled near Salem. He was Pappy's cousin, having married Uncle Natty's sister, Docia. They knowing this train had started and was getting in late, Mr. Herrin got on his horse and found us at this camp on the Sandy, sick and travel worn. Seeing our needs, he rode back home as quickly as he could and his brother, Noah, gathered supplies into the wagon and with good strong oxen come to our rescue, meeting us at Mr. Barlow's.

When we arrived at the Barlows, we drove up and camped right close to their home. Mr. Barlow came out to the camp and saw we were in great distress, many of us being sick. He said to father: 'Mr., I see you have a nice family and that you are in dire distress. Now I have a home, have plenty, and you are welcome to it. Go in and make yourself comfortable.'

"It was rainy season, about the first of December. We went right to his house. He had plenty of wood, a large fireplace and he said, "Now, you make your family just as comfortable as possible. If there is anything you have not got, say so. If you have no money that makes no difference. Keep an account of everything and when you do get some money you can pay me back." Father said he still had money and wanted to pay his way. Theodore and I were both very sick and were in the same wagon. As we drove up into camp Theodore said, "I'm going to get up." Mother said, "You are not able to get up." But he got up and fell over dead in the wagon. He was eight years old.

"In a few days, we pushed on to our destination at Salem Prairie where Mr. Herrin had rented a house for us. Here we spent most of the winter. This house was on the corner of Mr. Savage's farm.

Family Settles at
Salem Prairie

"Winter was on when we arrived in November. After we

were settled and over the fever we boys make lots of rails. There was much snow that winter. The Willamette River got so high that it flooded all of Salem.

"Later, in the winter, Pappy bought land joining Lute Savages and Mr. Z. Pollard. In 1856 or 1857, we boys bought the Pollard place and started raising apples and grain for the market. On this farm was a two story frame house. We had a visitor one day and he got the wrong plate at the table so we had to tell him we had turn-over plates. We got tired of batching and decided that some housekeepers would be nice to have.

Harvey Goes Off to War

"In 1855, I went to the Rogue River Indian War. Levi stayed on the farm and took care of the cattle. It was a hard winter with lots of snow and was intensely cold. We also owned a farm in Linn County with a log cabin on it and Levi had to ride horseback from Linn County to Salem feeding the stock at both places. I was away five months in this war. The same day I got my discharge from this company, I reenlisted to go to Walla Walla and Yakima to fight the Cayuse and Yakima Indians, who were murdering the stockmen and also they had killed one Indian Agent. On my first enlistment, to keep from freezing to death, we had to dig into the snow and wrap our one blanket around us to sleep. Shoes wore out and we had to wrap our feet in raw beef hides to keep the ice from cutting them.

"On the tenth day of June, 1858, I married Miss Perlina E. Wiloughby from near Poora, Linn County. A year later Levi married Miss Ediff Barger from near Harrisburg, Linn County.

Love of Nature & Sports
Brought Family to Molalla

"In 1860, Pappy traded the home he had bought two miles east of Salem for Mr. Charles Sweigles' donation land claim on the Molalla Prairie.

"Our Mother died there on Christmas Eve, 1865. She died suddenly of heart failure. She was well as usual and told all of the children to have dinner with them on Christmas Day. In the night a boy staying with them came for Levi and Ediff, who had bought the adjoining place, to tell them that Mother, as everyone called her, was dead. Mr. Reese one of the neighbors gave a plat of land for the burying place which is now called the Adams Cemetery, a beautiful; resting place over-looking the Molalla River with Mount Hood in the distance. Later Pappy had his two little sons, Aaron and Theodore, brought and laid to rest beside their mother.

"One of the characteristics of our family was the love of natural beauty and sports, such as hunting and fishing. When Pappy was 75, he chaperoned a party of 12 young folks, and drove one of the teams all the way to Salmon River Beach, a trip of three and a half days. When he was 80, one day he heard some hounds coming down the river so he took Levi's new single barrel shot gun which some of the hunters called, 'Levi's Pop Gun, only fit to kill crickets with'. He got there just in time to kill the first deer that came along and loaded again when the second one came up. He killed them both so saved the reputation of Levi's gun. Oliver was the real hunter of the family and can tell you many good stories of those times when game was plentiful here. In places where the fir grove are now monarchs, when we came to Molalla, deer heads could be seen above their tops. Pappy and all his sons were sure shots and even Jan could and did shoot birds. All had exciting adventures here in the early days when every shot had to spell death to the wild animals.

"Pappy died on February 15, 1895, and was placed beside his wife and two sons in the plat he had kept so nice all of those lonely years. His life was a busy and useful one from the time of his youth until his death at the age of 87 years.

"Uncle Natty Robbins was drowned in the Tualatin River at a mill dam, crossing over above the dam on a raft the pole being broken, proved to be too short to reach bottom and he being too old to swim went over and was lost. A Chinese boy on the raft with him swam ashore before they got into the swift current."

(This is the end of the family history written by Harvey Robbins in 1921.)

*   *   *

PART TWO:

"Robbins Brothers Store Pride of Molalla"

by Gail McCormick

In 1890, Levi Robbins and his son Oliver Willard purchased the general store along with the stock of $6,000 worth of goods at the Four Corners of Molalla. In 1905, Levi turned the store over to his sons to run and the store was named Robbins Bros. Co. By 1906, this store had become the pride of the Molalla prairie.

A 1906 edition of the Oregon City Courier describes Molalla at that time:

"Beautiful Molalla Prairie became one of the chief settlements in the very early history of Clackamas County. When eastern families come into this section, with its large fertile fields doted with splendid farm buildings and bearing a general air of prosperity, they are reminded of their eastern home. From the prairie one looks to the south and the east on the rolling foothills and just a little farther distant on the immense forests of fir, spruce and hemlock, a vast treasure that is soon to be poured into the channels of commerce. It is strange that transportation facilities have been withheld this long from a locality of such abundant resources. With the present impetus of railroad building in the west, however, Molalla has definite assurance of a railroad.

"In the heart of the prairie, Robbins Bros. Co. conduct a large general mercantile establishment. The proprietors, Levi Wayne Robbins, Everman Robbins and Frank E. Everhart, are young men of vim, energy and public

The Robbins Bros. Store was the pride of the Molalla prairie in the early 1900s. In 1907 the store did a business of $100,000.
All photos in the Robbins Bros. Store story are courtesy of Gena Cline.

enterprise. Their establishment is the pride of the community, carrying as they do, one of the largest and most varied stocks of general merchandise in the county and having for their patrons, people who appreciate this advantage. They may well lay the great part of their success to the loyal support of these people, who fully understand the value of such a home institution. Not only can the surrounding community purchase here, at reasonable prices, the needs of every day life, but it finds a market for farm products equivalent to that of the larger railroad towns.

"Such a business as this could never have been built up and could never have achieved it s present success had it not enjoyed in it s management the strictest integrity, energy and business ability. The young men conducting the Molalla store have grown up in the neighborhood from boyhood and it seems to be their chief pride to keep good the record of the old Molalla Corners, as one of the trading centers of Clackamas County. This is easily the largest interior trading point in the county.

"With the coming, in the near future, of railroad transportation, Molalla will become a keen rival for supremacy among the Clackamas County towns.

"As the center of the rich agricultural country surrounding it, the town will forge rapidly to the front. Mineral developments now rapidly going on a little way to the south and the great forests that are soon to pay their tribute to the uses of man will naturally accelerate the growth of Molalla.

"As fast as the Molalla country may forge to the front, the firm of Robbins Bros. Co. will keep in the vein. These young men represent the spirit of growth and progress. Loyal support of such men in the community is the key note of an advance all along the line."

Robbins Bros. store, at that time, was located near the intersections of Molalla Avenue and Main Street. In 1900, Oliver Willard had sold his interest in the store to his father and went into the carpentry industry. He is credited with

A reunion of the Robbins relatives at Levi Robbins home. Standing on porch from left: Ella Benson, unknown, Ediff Robbins, Levi Robbins, Philander Kayler, George Adams, Agnes Robbins, Ipha Robbins, Duane Robbins, Everman Robbins. Seated row 1: first four unknown, Winnie Kayler, Ivan Robbins, last two unknown. Row 2: Amanda Loveridge, Oliver Willard Robbins, Harvey Robbins, Kate Adams, Martha Kayler. Standing: Earl Kayler, Wayne Robbins, Annie Robbins, Newton Loveridge, Mr. Benson, Clara Robbins, Walter Beck. ca. 1920s.

Levi Wayne Robbins
1876 - 1971

Mrs. Levi Wayne Robbins - a classy looking lady indeed - and official buyer for the Robbins Bros. store in the 1920s was dubbed "Mrs. Molalla" at many of the 1920s Portland Buyers' Fairs.

building the Methodist Church and the First Molalla Bank in 1908, and also the spacious home occupied by his brother, Levi Wayne and his family. To his credit, these buildings still stand today.

Uncle Oliver Robbins, brother to Levi, Sr., bought 1,008 acres in 1865 about one mile south of Molalla and married Mary Jane Thompson the same year. She was a daughter to Robert Thompson, an early Marquam pioneer. Uncle Oliver and Aunt Mary were reportedly instrumental in getting the railroad into Molalla by putting $10,000 into the Willamette Valley Southern. The railroad arrived in Molalla in 1913. They also donated the city park and helped with other city improvements.

The 1920s were a prosperous time for the Robbins family. Ione Rivers Robbins, Levi Wayne's wife, was official buyer for the store. She attended many buyers' fairs in Portland and was dubbed "Mrs. Molalla" for her winning attitude about Molalla's positive qualities.

A 1924 Oregon Journal article describes the excitement she created at the Portland buyers' fair:

"Like a beam of sunshine on a drizzly day - Or like a cool breeze over the desert - Or like a hurricane at a quilting party - Or perhaps more like Emma McChesney come to life from the pages of Edna Ferber's book, breezed into the Portland Buyers' Week festivities the petite, frolicsome, vigorous little Mrs. Levi Wayne Robbins, buyer, champion prize winner, etc. etc. etc."

"She arrived from Molalla, Or., coming as official buyer for the Robbins Bros. general merchandise store of that city. She came as official buyer at the first Buyers' Week

Female swimmers at the Robbins' family reunion July 25, 1920. Top to bottom: Naomi Robbins, Mrs. Paul Robbins, Zella Shaver, Vivian Robbins, Shirley Robbins, Mrs. Arthur Benson and Robin Thayer.

Male swimmers at the Robbins' family reunion at Feyrer Park, July 25, 1920. Only identified is Duane Robbins, center on the left.

ever held in Portland - and this is the twelfth annual one. She hasn't missed one since.

"At each one, she's taken first prize ribbons home to show the home town folks. Her first prize was for having the most engaging smile of any guest at the first buyers' week. Next year she talked her way into honors in the oratorical contest. After the second or third year she just sort of grew into the nickname of 'Mrs. Molalla'."

Levi Wayne had married Ione Rivers in 1899. They had four children: Naomi, Leota, Vivian and Shirley.

In 1925, the store was sold to Molalla Mercantile Co., Inc. Those who served as clerks during the tenure of the store included family members Ipha Robbins and Frank Dicken.

After the sale of the store, Levi Wayne worked as head shipping clerk for Miller Brothers Store in Portland until he retired in 1964, at age 86. Continuing a family tradition of keeping active in old age, he went on to take second place in the National Oldtimers Golf Tournament in Chicago in 1969 when he was 92 years old!

Levi Wayne, along with his youngest brother, Everman, are credited with putting in the first telephone switchboard in Molalla in 1898 and the first telephone line to Oregon City in 1899.

In the 1920 s, huge family reunions were held at the Levi Wayne and Ediff Robbins' home and nearby Feyrer Park. Nearly all descendants of Jacob Robbins' and Nathanial Robbins' families attended. Much of the family genealogy was recorded by Ipha Robbins and through stories written and recorded for the reunions, such as the wagon train story by Harvey Robbins.

*   *   *

CHAPTER XIV

The Shavers of Molalla

"W.A. Shaver's Risky Ventures Proved Worthy" . . . . by Gail McCormick

W. A. Shaver sold the first carload of cattle in Clackamas county at 7 cents per pound. Twenty five animals were sold to Union Meat Company for $2200. W. A. Shaver is the second man from the left. ca. 1913. *All photos in the Shaver story are courtesy of Gena Cline.*

Bibliography:

Author Unknown, "W. A. Shaver", Morning Enterprise, July 15, 1915, Anniversary Edition
Cline, Gena of Molalla, Oregon, Unrecorded Interview, March, 1991
"Alfred Shaver" Portrait & Biographical Record of the Willamette Valley, Chapman Pub., 1903

"W. A. Shaver's Risky Ventures Proved Worthy"

by Gail McCormick

The first imported stallion brought into the Molalla area was a risky venture undertaken by W. A. Shaver in the early 1900s. He had tried to interest others in sharing this venture with him by attempting to form an association amongst the farmers for the purpose of breeding fine draft horses. Before the days of mechanization, draft horses were highly prized to assist with farm work. After repeated failures to enthuse others to this cause he

William Arthur Shaver
1868 - 1933

Della Gena Robbins Shaver
1873 - 1965

undertook the venture on his own initiative, taking all the chances himself. He is credited with being the pioneer in that line. A prize winning stallion, Zenophone, was purchased at the Lewis and Clark Fair in 1905. No colts were raised from this stallion as it died in Oregon City on its way to Molalla. But another colt, Bauces, proved to be a winner, and was the sire of many colts that brought as

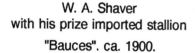

W. A. Shaver
with his prize imported stallion
"Bauces". ca. 1900.

high as $300 to $400 each in the open market.

William Arthur Shaver was a man of progressive ideas and had the courage to carry them out. At a time when most farmers were saying that land had become too valuable to raise beef on, "Bill" Shaver was making a comfortable fortune in the business. It was W. A. Shaver who sold the first carload of cattle in Clackamas County at seven cents per pound, the twenty five animals being sold to the Union Meat Company for $2200.00. He was probably the largest breeder of beef cattle in Clackamas County, selling 100 to 200 head of cattle each year from his 500 acre farm one mile west of Molalla. The 250 to 300 head of cattle kept on hand were pastured in the summer months in the mountains about twenty miles away. In the fall they were brought to the home ranch and fed during the winter.

In the early 1900s, Mr. Shaver was also the first man to bring a modern threshing outfit into the Molalla Valley. About 200 acres of his home ranch was farmed in general crops.

Born in the Waldo Hills area near Salem in 1868, William Arthur Shaver was brought to the Glad Tidings area, 3 miles north of Marquam as a boy. He grew up there on his father's farm and later attended Willamette College. He taught for a few years before marrying Della Gena Robbins. His father gave him a part of the Teasel Creek land he owned and there Bill and Della built a small house. In 1898, after his father had passed away, Bill decided to rent Jacob Robbins farm in Molalla which consisted of 640 acres. Bill and Della, with children Leo and Zella, moved to Molalla in the fall of 1899. He raised 250 plus head of cattle, 100 to 175 hogs, 250 sheep, 100 goats and 25 to 30 horses. He also bought a ranch on the middle and south fork of the Molalla River giving him free outside range for his cattle in the summer months. On this ranch in the mountains, which became known as the "Bee Ranch," he pastured his cattle in the summer months and kept one man busy with 100 stands of bees.

In 1905 he bought a sawmill on Woodcock Creek and ran it for several years. It was sold in 1910.

Grandfather came from Germany

W. A. Shaver's grandfather was George Washington Shaver, Sr.. George Shaver was born in Germany and his father lived to be 116 years old. The Shaver sons and their father were in several wars in Germany before George and his wife Margaret immigrated to America. They settled in Kentucky where sons George Washington Shaver, Jr. and Alfred Henry Shaver were born. Eventually they moved to Missouri where they owned a large farm with slaves. It was here that George Washington Shaver, Sr., passed away at the age of eighty years.

In 1849, George Washington Shaver, Jr., followed the migration to the gold mines of California. He didn't strike it rich so came on to Oregon and tried his hand at mining. He met and married Sarah Dixon, a woman from a prominent Portland pioneer family and they went on to found Shaver Transportation of Portland.

Threshing crew on the W. A. Shaver farm near Molalla, early 1900s.

Alfred Successful Miner

In 1850, Alfred set out from Missouri with ox teams and wagons and headed for the mines of California. He was fairly successful and in 1854, with some friends, came to Oregon, intending to return to his former home in Missouri. However, his brother insisted on his staying in Oregon, so he purchased some land and settled in the beautiful Waldo Hills near Silverton. Being still a young man and the wanderlust in his blood, he soon rented out this property and went to Boise City, Idaho, and engaged in teaming. He returned to Oregon in 1864.

Alfred Settles Down

On a visit to his brother's home he met and fell in love with Margaret Elizabeth Ridings. She had been working for George and Sarah by caring for their children. Alfred and Margaret married April 22, 1867, when she was twenty three and he was thirty years old.

They lived on the farm in Waldo Hills until William Arthur and sister Mamie (m. Charley Thomas) were born. In 1866, he bought 320 acres of land comprising the G. W. Jackson donation claim in the Glad Tidings district three miles north of Marquam, to which he added by later purchase until he finally owned 900 acres. Here he farmed and raised horses and four more children were born: Lulu (m. Charley Scott), Edgar (m. Nora Lebo),

Wava (never married) and Zoe (m. George Daugherty). In the meantime he sold the Waldo Hills farm.

He became a prominent man in Oregon, after settling down in a permanent location and held many positions of trust and responsibility in the community. He filled some political offices, as a Democrat, including that of road supervisor and school director.

Alfred Devoted to Horse Raising

In his younger days, Alfred was devoted to horse raising and during his entire life was the friend and admirer of the horse. Alfred and Margaret's granddaughter, Zella Shaver, wrote in a family history that "her grandfather was quiet and easy spoken. Grandmother loved to talk and play jokes on people and was always full of life. She loved to have her grandchildren with her and the more noise they made playing the more she liked it. She would say "she knew they were having a good time". Alfred and Margaret donated land in the Teasel Creek District for a Methodist Church and a camp meeting grounds in a grove with a large spring on the corner of their place. The church was built around 1867 and the last time it was used was for a wedding in 1918.

Interesting family stories passed down through the generations about the Glad Tidings farm. When Mamie was a baby, Alfred and Margaret got a Newfoundland dog to keep track of William when he was outside. One day

Margaret heard William screaming down by the creek, so she put the baby in the cradle and went to see what was happening. When she got down to the bank of the creek she could see the dog had William by the back of his clothes. He was wet all over. The dog had pulled him from the creek and he was mad at the dog! Later that summer, Margaret was working in her garden by the creek and William and Mamie were playing by the basket. The dog scared a deer and it jumped over the fence at Margaret. She hit it with her hoe and killed it.

Alfred passed away in 1898 and Margaret in 1909. Both are buried in the Adams Cemetery in Molalla.

W. A. and Della Shaver had five children; Leo Arthur, (b. 1894, m. Ethel Poulson), Zella (b. 1896, m. Frank F. Muller), Alfred Henry (b. 1901, m. Minnie Rosencrantz), Edith (b. 1904, m. Wayne Wright) and James William (b. 1911, m. Alice Miller).

What happened to the big farm of W. A. Shaver? Well, as fate would have it, after W. A. Shaver passed away, his son Leo tried to keep the holdings together. He was fatally injured in an auto accident in 1933 and over the intervening years the holdings have been sold.

* * *

The exquisite dress, style and figure of the turn-of-the-century woman is exemplified in this portrait of the Robbins sisters: Lida Nettie, Della Gena and Sara Martha. ca. 1900. Della Gena Robbins later became the wife of W. A. Shaver.

CHAPTER XV

The Hoffmans of Needy

"Hoffman's Stump Jack Does Work of Three Men" . . . by Gail McCormick

Hoffman's Lifting

AND

Logging Jack.

HOFFMANN'S LOGGING JACK

This Jack is similar to the Stump Jack, only lighter and more compact. It weighs only 38 pounds and is 24 inches high. It is built from the same materials as the heavier Jack and on the same principles. It is designed especially for loggers, house-movers and bridge-builders, who have found it superior to and other Jack on the market, as it can be used on three sides, where ordinary Jacks can be used only on one. In proportion to its size and weight its lifting capacity is much greater than that of any other Jack. See testimonials from loggers and house-movers. It is also very useful to have on a farm and will pay for itself in a short time. Price $20.00.

If there are no agents in your locality write to

Bibliography:
Author Unknown, "Blacksmith Invented Stump Jack," *The Bulletin*, March 14, 1979
Author Unknown, "Blacksmith in Needy, Oregon Held Patent," *The Bulletin*, September 12, 1979
Hoffman, Melvin, Unrecorded Interview, September, 1991
Yoder, Jim, "A History of Needy, Oregon," Published Manuscript, 1990

"Hoffman's Stump Jack Does Work of Three Men"

by Gail McCormick

In 1903, Charles Gottlieb Hoffman, a blacksmith and wagon maker from Needy, Oregon, patented a combined lifting jack and stump puller. He manufactured the stump jack in his blacksmith shop at Needy and sold it through Will Bros. in Aurora and Honeyman Hardware Co. in Portland, Oregon. He also patented a lifting and logging jack similar to the stump jack. The patents were carried in both the United States and Canada and were never sold.

Charles Hoffman's family came from Germany. After landing in New York, he settled in the Needy area to be close to German relatives residing in the Aurora area. Charles and Amelia Hoffman were married around 1900 and had a large family of ten children: Elma (m. Arthur Potter), Myra (m. Martin Rehm), Ida (m. Lloyd Barstad), Elsie (m. Irving Prather), Mabel (m. Lowell Hoblett), Harold Michael (never married), Kenneth (m. Alice Kirster) and Melvin (m. Edna Akes). Two other children, Elmer and Oscar, died as children.

The following testimonials were given regarding Mr. Hoffman's stump jack:

"Butteville, Oregon, February 16th, 1904.
Messrs. Will Bros., Aurora, Oregon.
Gentlemen: - In regard to yours of recent date regarding the Hoffman Stump Jack, will say it is the best Jack and has more power than any other hand machine I ever saw used.
Yours truly, James F. Kinyon"

"Albany, Oregon, March 6th, 1904.
Will Bros., Aurora, Oregon.
Gentlemen: - Yours of recent date at hand. In reply would say that the Stump Jack I bought of you is all right. I have made good use of it this winter. I did think I could sell a few around here, but it seems people want something that will do the work without an effort on their part. A number that could make good use of one of them

Charles Gottlieb and Amelia Hoffman
_1860 - 1928 * 1880 - 1964_
On their wedding day. ca. 1900

HOFFMAN'S STUMP
AND
LIFTING JACK.

(Patented.)

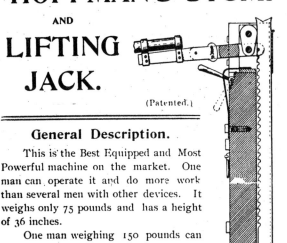

No. 723,155.   PATENTED MAR. 17, 1903.

C. G. HOFFMANN.
COMBINED LIFTING JACK AND STUMP PULLER.
APPLICATION FILED MAY 9, 1901.

NO MODEL.

General Description.

This is the Best Equipped and Most Powerful machine on the market. One man can operate it and do more work than several men with other devices. It weighs only 75 pounds and has a height of 36 inches.

One man weighing 150 pounds can raise 12000 pounds with a 10-foot lever. The lever is so constructed that it can be raised or lowered so that a long lever can be used at any place, thus increasing the power of the machine. These machines are tested to about twelve ton pressure, thus being impossible for one or two men to break them.

Construction: This machine is simple in construction and in case of a breakage parts can be procured at little expense. These machines are not only useful for clearing of land but there is not a farmer that has not some use for them daily. They can be used for raising all kinds of buildings and bridges. They are a great help to loggers to roll logs or to raise fallen trees that are lying in a twisted manner when you are sawing or for any place where such heavy lifting is needed.

Material: Hoffman's Stump and Lifting Jack is made of carefully selected materials. The lifting bar is made of the best tool steel, all bolts are of good steel and the wood work is made of the best seasoned Oregon oak, heavily lined with steel.

Advantages: One of the great advantages of this machine is that it can lift objects on the same level as the base of the Jack, but little digging being required to get below the stump or weight to be raised. It can be used in cramped quarters and in any position, and its light weight makes it easy to handle and move around. Price, $20.

Patent No. 723,155. Patented March 17, 1903.

Fig. 1.   Fig. 2.   Fig. 3.   Fig. 4.   Fig. 5.

Witnesses:
E. M. Howatson
F. W. Ayers

Inventor,
Charles G. Hoffmann.
by T. J. Geisler
Atty.

have been here and pronounced them a fine thing, but are not ready to buy just yet. However, I will do what I can for you.
Yours Respectfully, W. H. Foster"

"Portland Oregon, December 23, 1903.
Honeyman Hardware Co., Portland, Oregon.
Dear Sirs: - Two Hoffman Jacks that we bought from your house have given good satisfaction for light logging

purposes and particularly so for chute building. They are light and convenient for handling and can be used where other Jacks cannot be used at all. They have been in constant use for the past year with but very little repair.
Rocky Point Logging Co., by Ed McIntosh."

"Will Bros., Aurora, Oregon
Gentlemen: - Having used your Hoffman Stump Jack for

Charles Hoffman's Blacksmith Shop in Needy, Oregon, around 1901. Shoeing the horse is Charles Hoffman, while his daughter, Elma, is seated at the corner of the building. Two men at left are unidentified.
All photos in the Hoffman story are courtesy of Melvin Hoffman.

---

the past two years, I can say that it far surpasses anything of the kind yet gotten up. One man, with the aid of the Hoffman Jack, can take out stumps that three men could not handle without it. For an illustration I saw one stump pulled in my field, 32 inches in diameter, and after being turned out, measured 20 feet across the roots and stump, and this was done by two men and the Hoffman Jack, and it can be put to many other uses on the farm. Can be used as a wagon jack or log jack. For moving or raising buildings. I think they are superior to the jack screw.
Wishing you success with the Hoffman, I am,
Respectfully Yours, W. L. White"

"Portland, Oregon, December 23, 1903.
Will Bros., Aurora, Oregon
Dear Sirs: - In regard to the Hoffman Jack, I find it to be much superior to any other Jack of its style that I have ever used for strength. As I am in the house moving business and handle many different styles of Jacks, I can highly recommend the Hoffman Jack.
Yours truly, A. D. Moodie"

Over a period of time, the demand for the manually operated stump jack declined. Later, Charles and Amelia's sons, Mike and Melvin, operated a garage out of the same building the blacksmith shop was in.

* * *

by Jim E. Yoder

"The early 1900s saw Needy as a small, thriving community dating back to the pioneer settlers of the early 1950s. The first merchant, James S. Vinson, began business there about 1854. He later sold the business to the Rev. Jesse Moreland, who, according to Clackamas County postal records, was also Needy's postmaster from February 27, 1864 until December 7, 1873.

"Needy's post office was established February 16, 1855, with John M. Bacon serving as its postmaster until April 18, 1856, when a J. F. Walk took over. Over a half century and eleven subsequent postmasters, the post office was closed on September 10, 1908. Its demise being attributed to rural routes from communities which have grown to be larger centers.

"How Needy got its name is not without controversy. According to an "Oregonian" article by John S. Vinson, March 17, 1928, a James H. Brents, who was something of a humorist, noting that the county was rather rough and infertile, called the district "Hardscrabble" and named its trade center "Needy." George H. Himes told the compiler of "Oregon Geographic Names," that it wasn't the character of the soil, which was excellent, but the unfortunate condition of some pioneer settlers who lived there.

"There were several businesses operating in this busy little town. The building at far left housed a blacksmith shop in front and a woodshop behind where Hoffman stump jacks were produced. It was operated by Charles G. Hoffman, and later by his sons Harold and Melvin, as a garage. The Hoffman's house sat to the south and west of the shop. A general store, next to the blacksmith shop, had living quarters for its owners, a telephone switchboard, and a dance hall above. It was established in the late 1800s and operated by a Mr. Hardisty. The Albert Thompsons bought it in 1903 and operated it until around 1920. The two-story square house was the residence of Clarence Miller. He operated a confectionery and card room next door. The porch-fronted one-story building in the corner, was a general store and the Needy post office, operated by a Peter Cook. It was built by Sam Kauffman, and was already there when he moved to Needy in 1888. To the west of this building stood a livery stable. The last of the original town buildings was owned by the Rock Creek Odd Fellows Lodge. It was a two-story square building that housed a general store with living quarters on the lower level, and the Odd Fellows and Pansy Rebekahs' meeting hall above."

Publisher's note: The picture above is from a 1908 post card. Almost all of these buildings have been destroyed by fire over a period of time.

CHAPTER XVI

Ogle Mountain Mine

PART ONE: "There's Gold In Them Thar' Hills" by Gail McCormick
PART TWO: "J.V. Harless: Farmer, Prospector and Hunter"
. . . . Enterprise Courier, 9/15/1935

A tired mining crew rests at the opening to the upper tunnel of Ogle Mountain Mine. ca. 1910.

Bibliography:
Author Unknown, "Ogle Mountain Mine Boomed in '13," <u>The Bulletin</u>, September 28, 1983 & December 26, 1973
Author Unknown, "Ogle Mountain Mine Under Production," <u>Molalla Pioneer</u>, October 11, 1934
Author Unknown, "J. V. Harless Sowed First Clover," <u>Oregon City Enterprise</u>, Sunday, September 15, 1935
Harless, Mildred, Unrecorded Interview, September, 1991
Hardy, Charles, "Ogle Mountain Mine," <u>Early History of Molalla & Nearby Areas</u>, 1969
Hemphill, Tony L., "Ogle Mountain Mining Times," <u>The Ogle Genealogist, Vol. 5</u>, 1984
Lynch, Vera M., "Early Mining Stories," <u>Free Land for Free Men</u>, 1973

PART ONE:

"There's Gold in Them Thar' Hills"

by Gail McCormick

Gold in Clackamas County! Yes, but don't rush out and buy a gold pan and shovel until you read the rest of the story . . .

In 1860, a California gold miner named William Sprague was hired by a hopeful group of business men comprising the Oregon City Inc. Mining Company. He discovered gold in the Molalla River basin. The gold he found assayed out at $695 a ton. He quickly returned to the mining company with the good news only to find that the company was dissolved due to lack of capital. On his own Sprague set up a claim and started surface digging and netted $3 to $5 a day. He had worked the claim for only a brief time when a Chinese miner named Wa Kee offered him $150 for it. Sprague sold but, due to a residency law that prohibited a Chinese person or a Negro to set up residence and own a business in the state, Wa Kee had to give up his enterprise. This claim was thought to be along Lost Coffee Creek.

The hint of gold at their doorsteps aroused the interest of two brothers, Howard and Robert Ogle, enough that they gave up their businesses in Molalla and scurried to the hills to take up prospecting. In 1862, they found gold in the creek that bears their name - Ogle Creek.

It didn't take long for the word to spread and people from all over the Willamette Valley began saturating the major river systems in search of their fortunes. Salem area residents searched in the Santiam River, while those nearer to Portland searched the Clackamas River basin. In south Clackamas County, a search was on for the "mother lode" in the Molalla River.

By the mid-1880s, claims began dotting the Molalla River. Colorful names of mining claims began to tell the story of men with fortune on their minds; the Wildcat Lode, the Camelback Lode, the Swede, the Mary Gold, the Silver Star Lode, the Lucky Chance, the Golden Eagle, the Bonanza Lode, the Second Chance, the Accident Lode and the Silver Queen.

Henry Russell, an orphan adopted by the Russell family, grew up in Molalla. He was experienced in the gold

An impressive horseshoe shaped display of the ore from Ogle Mountain Mine was set up at the 1905 Lewis and Clark Exhibition in Portland, Oregon.
Photo courtesy of Mildred Harless.

business. His parents had moved to the Payette River Valley where he helped at an inn weighing out gold brought in by the Idaho gold miners in payment of their food, lodging and liquor. Around 1890, Henry and his wife

Nettie homesteaded an area along the Molalla River just below the junction of Table Rock Creek and the South Fork of the Molalla River. There they set up a bee ranch with over 100 hives. From this home base, he took to the hills prospecting, exploring and hunting. He also aided the government surveyors in surveying the Molalla River Basin and did timber cruising in the area.

Russell Hits Rich Gold Pocket

In June of 1894, a rich grass roots pocket of free gold was struck by Henry Russell and Charlie Pelkey. The gold was an oxidized material having free and wire gold fully visible and easily obtainable. Henry Russell, using only a candle holder, filled a pint Mason Jar in one day. This pocket was assayed at over $2000 a ton and the word spread fast of the richest strike yet on Ogle Creek.

Over 150 claims were filed at Clackamas County Courthouse within the period between 1894 and 1908 as Ogle Mountain began to crawl with weekend prospectors. Most claims were filed in the Ogle Creek and Copper Creek areas.

By 1903, people had grouped together to form corporations to mine the gold in south Clackamas County. Four companies formed; The East Portland Mining Company, a consolidation of placer claims along the South Fork of the Molalla River; The Molalla Central Mining Company, a consolidation of lode claims along the Table Rock Fork of the Molalla River; The Clackamas Mining and Milling Company, a consolidation of claims on the east side of Ogle Mountain; and the most ambitious of the companies, Ogle Mountain Mining Company, a consolidation of claims along Ogle Creek.

Henry Russell sold his claims to the Ogle Mountain Mining Company, organized by Al and John Fairclough of Oregon City. The Fairclough set up their offices in Oregon City and chose as their shipping point Scotts Mills, Oregon. They brought out samples of the ore and began to solicit capital for their exploits. They issued $1,000,000 capital stock at par value of $1 per share. Soon the stock was all sold and plans were made to build a quartz mill to process the rich ore. Other attempts to promote the mining venture included an impressive horseshoe shaped display of rich ore from Ogle Mountain Mine displayed at the 1905 Lewis and Clark Exhibition in Portland, Oregon. This brought statewide notice and strong support from local residents.

Road Cut Through Forest

In 1904, a road from Scotts Mills to the mine site was cut through the Douglas Fir forests. Equipment for the mill was shipped into the mines by mule train in 1905 from Scotts Mills. The road ended at a steep pitch below the mine and the teams had to be unhitched and the wagons pulled up and let down with block and tackle.

Charles Hardy, who did a little mining himself, in his "Early History of Molalla and Nearby Areas" describes some problems the miners encountered: (He was delivering mail to the mine.)

"Boyles and I would go to the Joe Davis cabin, or as lots of folks called it, the Dungeon, and leave our horses there and cross the river on a big drift in the river, and then go up Butcher Knife Mountain to the mines. Sometimes the snow was pretty deep when we got pretty well up Butcher Knife Ridge. They were sure glad to see us when we came, and we were glad to see them too when we were about tired out in the snow. So it was a glad bunch.

"We had to follow the trail by the blazes on the trees. There was so much snow that there was no trail to be seen. We knew what we were up against when we started, so we took sleeping bags in case we had to lay out in the snow.

"The Fairclough sold stock in the mine to finance the expense of road building and machinery, and moving it in which was a big job. We did not have any gas machinery at that time such as trucks and bulldozers. All work had to be done with horses and wagons. They came by way of Scotts Mills. When they got to the end of the road they had to build their own road. Some of the machinery was quite heavy for to be handled on wagons and such kind of roads that you can't imagine the trouble they had moving in. When they got within about one mile of the mine they had a hill to go down that was so steep that they had to put a cable around the hind axle and anchor to trees to let it down. The marks of the cable on the trees are to be seen yet today. They moved in a 5-stamp mill rock crusher, steam engine, and a little sawmill. Later on they moved in a smelter.

"They had many problems to be solved. Now the stamp mill had to be set up where there was water so, they put it down at Ogle Creek. The mine was up on a very steep ridge and when I say steep ridge I mean steep. You had to hold on to the brush to pull yourself up or let yourself down some 500 to 600 feet to the mine. Now the problem was to get the ore down to the mill. First they built a log trough to slide the ore down. But the ore or rock would not slide. They would roll and get up such speed that they would jump out of the trough. So next they covered the trough, but the rocks would knock the cover off.

"Now working on a hill so steep that you had to hold on to brush to go up and down made all that work very difficult and slow. So then they built an aerial tram as they called it. Two cables stretched a little way apart and they had trolleys or buckets on them to carry the ore down to the mill. There were brakes on each of the

"They came by way of Scotts Mills.. and you can't imagine the trouble they had moving in...they were most of the summer getting that tube moved.." *Photo courtesy of Mildred Harless.*

cables so that the tram could be operated from the mine. The loaded bucket when it went down would pull the empty bucket back to the mine. Now the getting of the ore down to the mill was pretty well solved, but the next difficulty was entirely different. When the ore was crushed as fine as they could get it, only about half of the gold would fall out, what we call free milling ore to be picked up by the quicksilver plates behind the stamps, and the other half would go out in tailing behind and was lost. Now they could not stand for that and the only solution was to put in a smelter so they could get all the gold.

"Now a smelter tube is a very heavy thing and cannot be taken apart, had to go in one piece. They were most all one summer getting that tube moved into the mine and set up ready for use, and low and behold fate seemed against them. The first batch they used it on they spoiled the cyanide that is used in connection with a smelter.

Now they got this cyanide from Germany and it was very expensive. They all were so disgusted that there has not been much done with the mine since."

But it was more than the cyanide error that brought about the downfall of the mining venture. While the mill was being built, men began pushing tunnels deep into the bowels of Ogle Mountain. The mines were at an elevation of four thousand feet, so they could only be worked in the summer months. The air in the upper mine became bad and it was too far from the mill to pump air into the mine, so mine employees began pushing a portal upward to the surface. They worked hard and were continuously being plagued with oxygen depleted air. Their biggest problem was keeping the candles from going out due to lack of oxygen. Finally they broke through at the base of a hemlock where air began gushing through the mine creating a five mile per hour breeze.

Mill Completed

The summer of 1908 the mill was completed and the lower mining camp grew to consist of a quartz mill, saw mill, tunnel house, dynamite shack, assay office, business office, cookhouse-guest house, three bunkhouses and two storage buildings. In order to obtain maximum working hour efficiency, an upper tunnel camp was constructed consisting of a blacksmith building, cookhouse and bunkhouse.

Men lived at the upper mine during the week and lived at the lower camp only on weekends. From the years 1903 to 1910 the upper mine tunnel was heavily mined. The tunnel into the mountain reached 400 feet, where it branched into two more tunnels - one 100 feet and

A mill camp sprung up on the side of Ogle Mountain. From the left; Mrs Heckert, cook, John Fairclough, general manager, Mrs. John Fairclough, cook and Jim Hatton, foreman of the mines. ca 1908. *Courtesy of the Molalla Historical Society.*

Ogle Mountain ore cart on display at the Dibble House in Molalla. The cart was donated by Sid Gasser. *Photo from the author's collection.*

another 200 feet deep. Mine carts were run along rails constructed of two-by-fours with cast iron strips on the contact surface. (One of these ore carts is on display at the Dibble House in Molalla.) All lighting in the upper tunnel consisted of candles hung from timbers in special mining candle holders.

Small Town Develops
During these productive years, the population of Ogle Creek Camp reached 100 men and women. The mill camp was imperative to the mining operation as the ore had to be processed after it was mined. A complex interlocking system was used for power with the main operation powered by steam produced by heat from three large wood burning boilers. The wood for the boilers was cut at the sawmill. The life of the camp depended on this power supply for the electricity used in the camp, the air in the lower tunnel and the ore processing equipment.

The ore coming from the mines was dumped into an ore bin and then through trap doors into two jaw crushers with 18-20 inch openings. Then the ore went through a three process sort system consisting of passing the ore over a finely meshed screen that passed the fine powder and free gold onto a shaker table with riffles to extract the free gold from the fine powder. The free gold then passed through to the amalgamation process and the fine powder was sent to the cyanide process.

The main body of ore, which was in chunks, was sent from the sorter to the stamp mill. The stamp mill was a set of iron plates with a system of piston-like iron stamps that crushed the ore into a sand-like powder when dropped onto it. From the stamp mill, the ore was transferred to a large iron cylinder five feet by twenty feet. The ore was dumped into this cylinder, along with some quartzite boulders imported from the Canby area. These boulders were tube shaped. The cylinder rotated and the boulders (tubes) pulverized the ore into a fine powder.

The cyanide process used consisted of three cylindrical vats filled with strong, medium and weak liquor in that order. The ore was transferred from the strong to the weak solution in a leaching process that took three to fourteen days. The liquor was then pumped into precipitation boxes and passed over zinc filings that turned into a black slime. This slime was treated with sulfuric acid that dissolved excess zinc leaving only gold slime that was then washed and dried and sent to amalgamation.

The amalgamation process consisted of a series of copper plates fed with mercury.

Mining Versus Timber Rights
In 1907, after all this work, just when the future had begun to look rosy someone filed an application for the timber rights on Ogle Mountain. The U. S. Land Department attempted to sell the land without notifying the hard working Ogle Mountain Mining Company! An attorney for the Ogle Mountain Mining Company read of the action in the newspaper and immediately filed a complaint and the mining company soon found themselves in court.

At that time, the court gave the mining company the rights to the lands as mineral lands but this did not end the battle. In 1908, application again was made for timber rights and again the Ogle Mountain Mining Company won. But many small, neighboring, independent mining claims were being abandoned as the independent miners did not have such a large investment in their enterprises as the Ogle Mountain Mining Company and soon Ogle Mountain Mining Company stood alone on the hill.

Mining Engineers Make Grave Errors
Then the mining engineers shifted their full efforts into sinking a horizontal shaft at mill level to hasten the transportation of the ore. This proved to be a grave error as the ore at that level was very low in gold and silver. They had expended their money in labor and digging further into the mountain with the hope of hitting more of the rich veins found in the upper tunnel. They failed.

The enterprise was expensive and capital was getting low so the mining engineer suggested eliminating the stamping process and selling the stamp mill for additional capital. This also proved to be a mistake and the mines limped along until 1914, when trouble in Europe threatened to put an end to badly needed mining supplies purchased from Great Britain. Ogle Mountain Mine was shut down in 1915.

Efforts Futile to Revive Mine

After the war was over, Ogle Mountain Mining Company leased its holdings for two years to William C. Daly, a Molalla prospector. He removed considerable amounts of gold and silver during that time.

In 1920, the mines again were threatened by timber claims, but rather than fighting it in the courts, they made safe their claims by purchasing the land from the Federal Land Office. However, the mine was not worked between 1920 and 1934 due to lack of capital.

In 1934, M. E. Kruger and D. A. Edlin of Portland hired a force of eleven men and tried to revive the mine. Their effort failed when their capital ran out and any hope of reviving the mine seemed lost.

In 1953, the acting president of the Ogle Mountain Mining Company sold the land to Weyerhaeuser Timber Company.

*   *   *

PART TWO:

"J.V. Harless:

Farmer, Prospector and Hunter"

The following is reprinted from the Oregon City Enterprise, September 15, 1935. Author unknown.

"Most all the old pioneers, as the fancy or necessity struck them, were by turns, farmers, hunters or prospectors. Hunting and prospecting usually go hand in hand, and that each has its peculiar fascination no one will deny. It matters little how many deer a man may have killed, he always hopes the next one will be the largest. And the prospector is always looking forward to the strike that will make him independent.

"J. V. Harless, of whom this story is written, was no exception to the rule, and was all three by turns, farmer, prospector, hunter. He experienced the thrill of watching things grow, and among those growing things, he holds the record of having sowed and reaped the first field of clover ever raised in Clackamas County. They laughed at him and told him that clover would not grow in this country. We haven't anything to say to this except that Oregon now produces some of the finest clover in the world.

"He experienced the thrill of hunting, along with the

Joseph Vinton & Etta Adams Harless
with daughter Golda (Edmondson)
ca. 1915
Photo courtesy of Mildred Harless

greater thrill of prospecting, of which more will be told later on in my story.

"Mr. Harless was born in Anderson, Indiana, and came to Oregon in March of 1877. He arrived a little late to be called one of the early pioneers, but was a pioneer nevertheless. He owned the first steam traction engine in this part of the country. Mr. Harless told me that every time the engine blew off steam the farmers would drop their pitchforks and run for their lives. For which they could hardly be blamed, because those old engines had a habit of blowing up and scattering pieces of metal all over the map.

"On the tenth of May, two months after he arrived in Oregon, Mr. Harless and his father (Jake Harless) moved to Salem. Evidently Salem was just Salem to the elder Harless, because in the fall of '77 they moved back to Molalla where they lived for a while on the Jordan place, then they moved back to Indiana. No doubt Indiana had lost its former appeal because they came back to Oregon again in March of 1880. This time they made preparations to stay by buying Matt Hamilton's old home, and with it they secured Matt's pioneer, hand-made flour bin which to this day is still in use.

"They lived on the Hamilton place 13 years and while there cured meat for all the old timers. Some of the old timers, among them the Elys, still pleaded with Mr. Harless to cure meat for them. Then in 1902 they bought the old Saunders place which was built by a German named Heines in 1882.

"When the Harless family first came to Molalla there were just two stores and one blacksmith shop, and all the grain raised in that part of the county was hauled to Oregon City for sale or shipment. The first telephone exchange in Molalla possessed a switchboard with just three plugs. It is still there, but fortunately not now in use.

"Mr. Harless became interested in mining in 1896, and staked several claims on Henline Creek in a big body of low grade ore. He said he drove a tunnel in Henline Mountain full 200 feet through hard rock.

"In 1903 he became interested in the Ogle mining property. Howard Ogle, for whom Ogle Mountain was named, found the first gold there in 1862, but it remained for Henry Russell to make the first real strike. The gold in the Ogle Mine is quite often free, and the ore assays as high as $200 a ton. Harless has one of the finest collections of minerals in the state."

Author's note: Joseph Vinton Harless married Etta Adams. Their children were Fenton (b. 1908, m. Mildred), Lyle, Golda (m. Norman Edmonson) and Val.

*   *   *

CHAPTER XVII

Mulino, Oregon

– A Step Back in Time

"The Howards of Mulino" . . . . by Gail McCormick

This photo of the road to Mulino in 1928 shows Howard's Grist Mill on the left and the Waldorf Blacksmith Shop on the right. The first blacksmith shop was the small frame building directly south of the Mill. Howard's Grist Mill today is pictured in the inset and is documented as the oldest industrial building standing in Oregon today. *Bottom photo is courtesy of the Oregon Historical Society. All photos of the Mulino buildings as they stand today are from the author's collection.*

Bibliography
Almond, Nellie Waldorf, Recorded Interview, June, 1991
Author Unknown, "Ed Howard Interview," Molalla Pioneer, November 7, 1946
Author Unknown, "Mulino, A New Townsite," Morning Enterprise, Anniversary Edition, 1912
Author Unknown, "Mulino Store Community Institution," The Bulletin, February 19, 1975
Clackamas County Directory, "Mulino," 1916
Clarke Publishing Co., "Bayne A. Howard," History of Columbia River Valley, 1928
Dix, Lillian Waldorf, Unrecorded Interview, August, 1991
Engle, Blanche Daniels, Recorded Interviews, April & September, 1991
Engle, Blanche, "First Mulino Settlers Build Mills," The Bulletin, April 11, 1973
Harry, DeWitt, "Grist Mill of Pioneers," The Oregonian, April 23, 1922
Hostetler, Barbara Howard, Unrecorded Interview, October, 1991
Jones, Fran, "137 Year-Old Mulino Mill," The Oregonian, March 23, 1982
Lyttle, John W., "Mulino Graveyard," Published Manuscript, 1980
Maben, Roberta, "Mulino Grange Celebrated 100th Year," Oregon Grange Bulletin, June 3, 1985
Williams, Frank, "First Settlers to Mulino in 1845," Published Manuscript, Date Unknown

"*The Howards of Mulino*"

by Gail McCormick

One hundred and forty five years ago, Oregon was virgin territory. It was 1843 and the great migration from the east had just started headed for the Oregon territory. Land was free for the claiming and families were willing to make sacrifices to follow their dream of a new home out west. Richard Rutter Howard, a skilled miller, was sparked with the dream and with his family, including six children, he crossed the Oregon Trail in 1845. His dream lives on today in the form of Howard's Grist Mill, documented as the oldest industrial building standing in Oregon today.

Oregon had become a territory of hardy bands of men and women scattered throughout. Food was a main necessity and a good miller was needed to provide flour for the early settlers. Almost all the pioneers that traveled the Oregon Trail culminated their trip at Oregon City. Thus Oregon City became headquarters for the new territory and Clackamas County was settled early on.

Richard Rutter Howard was born November 18, 1797, in Shelbyville, Maryland, in Howard County. The county was named after an early ancestor. Richard had been bonded out in his early boyhood to learn the trade of saw milling and flour milling. The Howard family then moved to Illinois, and then to Ohio. It was while living in Ohio that Richard met and married Cynthia Turner, born October 19, 1810. She lived in the neighboring state of Kentucky.

Perfect Homesite Found

When the family arrived in Oregon, Richard Howard, with his dream, scoured the territory south of Oregon City on horseback searching for the perfect place to set up his mill. Although he traveled as far south as Silverton, he kept returning to the little winding stream, naturally crooked into an oxbow and surrounded by huge cedar trees ten miles south of Oregon City. The Indians had named the stream "Nazzic Cu-Nazzic" creek, which meant "Squawking Duck". Nearby was a perfect meadow to build a cabin for his family. With his decision easily made, he returned to Oregon City to file a. donation land claim

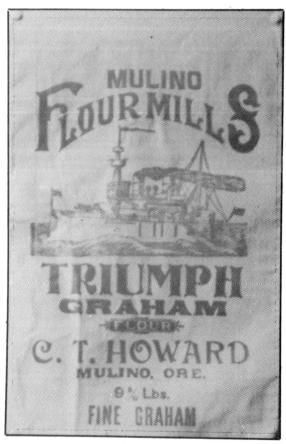

A Howard's Grist Mill flour sack.
From the collection of Alvin Friedrich.

of six hundred forty acres which spread all over what is now Mulino and as far south as the Molalla River. Later he renamed the little winding stream Milk Creek.

A tent was set up and Richard R. Howard brought his large family to the spot of his dreams in the spring of 1846. In the fall, their ninth child, Anna was born in the tent. Soon, a one room log cabin was built and in 1848, a saw mill was built to provide lumber for the other buildings soon to arise.

Howard's Grist Mill Built

In 1851 the Howard's Grist Mill was built of twelve inch hand hewn timbers and square nails. Those great timbers have withstood the test of time and still stand today in proud acclamation of Richard Rutter Howard's skill. At that time both mills used water for power. A dam was built across Milk Creek upstream and south of the mill. Just north of the mill, across the road that we now know as Highway 213, a large canal was dug in a most unusual way. First they built an earthen dam and headgates across the creek. Then they plowed a lane with oxen where they wanted the mill race to be. They opened the gates and flooded the lane, and the fresh-plowed loose dirt was washed down stream. Then they plowed the lane another plow's-depth, and flushed it down stream. After proceeding in this manner several times they had a mill race dug. A head gate was installed so the flow of water could be increased or decreased as needed.

The burrs for the grist mill, bought in New York City, were sent around Cape Horn and did not reach their destination until a year after the order was placed. The shafting and wheels were of wood and the flour sacks were made by hand by Richard's wife, Cynthia.

At that time, flour from the McLoughlin mills cost twenty-five cents a pound but Richard R. Howard charged only sixteen to eighteen cents and had more orders than he could fill. He paid five dollars a bushel for wheat in the early days, when gold dust was plentiful and the price of all commodities was high.

Pack Trains Came From Gold Mines

In 1851 and 1852 pack trains came from the mines in northern California and from the southern Oregon diggings near Jacksonville to load up with flour at Howard's Mill. Two or three barrels were ground in an hour and by working twenty-four hours between fifty and sixty barrels were turned out in a day. The biggest run ever made in twenty-four hours was seventy-two barrels. The two principal brands of flour were "Howard's Blend", which was made from a blended wheat, and "Hard Wheat Patent", made from the best quality of hard wheat shipped from eastern Oregon and Washington, no hard wheat being produced in the Willamette Valley. Bleaches were nearly unknown and most flour was wheat and buckwheat. In those days, each farmer would turn his grain into the mill to be ground and wait long hours for his own grist for each one considered his a superior product.

Howard Family Continues to Grow

By 1854 the Howard family had grown to ten children:
Francis T., William, John, Sarah, Charles Turner, Daniel Boone, Mary, Grace, Anna, and Anthony Wayne. That year a new home was built across the bridge to the west of the mill. It was also made of hewn logs and lumber from the Howard's Mill. This stately old Howard home was large with a full front veranda adorned with four white columns. It had an old-fashioned kitchen, a dining room, a study with a fireplace and shelves to hold many books. There was a parlor with large bay windows looking to the east toward the mills. The upstairs held five bedrooms leading off the main hallway and a master bedroom. On the back of the house was a stone cellar, a well for water and other outbuildings, including a wood shed. (This house was torn down in the 1930s.) Two big barns were built - one for the horses and one for the cows. Men were hired to help with the farm work and to haul grain and flour to and from the mill. A wagon road led down the hill from the house across a covered bridge over Milk Creek leading to the grist mill.

Three generations of this same family operated the mill over the years. Charles T. Howard took over when his father passed away in 1865. He was educated in Clackamas County and received instruction from Lafayette May, who taught school in a log cabin owned by his brother Tom.

Mulino Community Named

Charles T. Howard is credited with changing the name of the town from Howard's Mill to Mulino. Mulino was first called Howard's Mill but in 1882, when the first post office was established, it became necessary to have an official name. Howard's Mill was put on the forms and returned to Washington D. C. It was rejected as being too long. Then Howard was suggested, only to find that there was another Howard in the eastern part of Oregon. Then the Spanish word Molino, meaning mill or mill by the stream, was submitted only to be refused because of the possibility of it being confused with Molalla. The spelling was changed to Mulino and it was accepted. The inspiration for Molino came from a Spanish miller who worked for Charles. The miller lived where the Ranch Hills Golf Course is now located and each morning as he would leave his home to go to the mill, he would say that he was going to Molino.

After his father's death Charles successfully continued the business gradually introducing new methods and modern appliances. He abandoned the old water wheel and installed three iron turbines, one of which supplied the plant with electric light. However water was still the motive power.

The second and third generation of Howards that operated Howard's Grist Mill. Seated in front are Mary Sanders Howard and Charles Turner Howard. Back row from left is their children Claude, Bayne and his wife Lillian Gans Howard. ca. 1908. *Photo courtesy of Barbara Howard Hostetler.*

C. T. and Mary Sanders Marry

Charles was married May 28, 1874, to Mary Hannah Sanders, who was born in 1853, on the North Howell prairie near Salem. Her parents, Asa and Abbie (Woodward) Sanders, came to Oregon with the pioneers of 1851 and located on a donation land claim on North Howell prairie. They proved up on the property and sold it in 1857. They then moved to Molalla and purchased part of the Sweigle donation land claim.

Charles and Mary lived their lifetime in Mulino and were instrumental in the development of the community. Charles was a charter member of the Mulino Grange and the first secretary of the organization. Founded in 1873, for three years the organization met in private residences. Then a grange hall was built by donated labor and lumber on land given by Peter Noyer, Sr. It was the only hall in the community and was used as a church, for public gatherings and for several years as a public schoolhouse.

This hall was located on what is now Darnell Road. This building no longer stands.

In the early 1900s, Mary Howard donated a bible to the grange in which she had written the names of the charter members; Peter Noyer Sr., Jane Noyer, Everett G. Noyer, Sophia Noyer, Peter S. Noyer, Delilah Noyer, John Noyer, Nancy Noyer, Jackson Knotts, Martha Knotts, J. G. Trullinger, Ellen Trullinger, Jesse Adkins, Ellen Adkins, Joseph Craig, Sarah Craig, James Officer, John Smith, Rev. John Darnell, C. T. Howard, Mary Sanders Howard, W. A. Jones, W. L. Bohna, D. N. Trullinger and B. Savage, Dr. Rueben Goucher, Catherine Goucher, C. A. Miller, John Payne and M. Ringo.

During the depression, the Grange sold the hall and grounds and purchased for the very nominal fee of $1 the present Grange hall for the Community Club. The old hall has a history in itself, at one time containing a meat market, store, barber shop and bath.

CLACKAMAS COUNTY DIRECTORY, 1916.   MULINO   163

Mt Pleasant Rose Society, Mrs A C Warner Pres, Ella E Williams Sec, Mrs W B Stafford Treas; meets at call of the president
Snook Grace, tchr Mt Pleasant Public School
Weivesick Cora, tchr Mt Pleasant Public School, Res Oregon City

MULINO

MULINO—Located 10 miles south of Oregon City on Milk creek and the Willamette Valley Southern Ry., which operates 5 trains daily to and from Oregon City. Has a church, modern graded school, large public hall and Grange hall. American Express Co., telephone connection with all parts of the county, flour and sawmill. Mulino is becoming an important shipping point and is the trading center for a rich tributary country which with the advent of the railway is rapidly developing. Rich soil well adapted for dairying, fruit growing and mixed farming makes this a desirable location.
Allen Donald L, carrier R F D 1
American Express Co, E B McConally agt
Berdin E P, billiards
Board of Education, Oscar Halt chairman, J Mallett Mrs. Mary Snodgrass directors, Vesta Churchill clerk
DANIELSON ALFRED (Lena), General Merchandise (See Adv)
Dougan Arthur, fruit and produce
Erickson A, propr Mulino Hotel
FISH THOS W (Viola), Fresh and Cured Meats (See Adv)
Grice Flora, teacher Mulino public school

Haynes C F, barber
Howard B A, sec-treas Mulino Water Co
HOWARD C T (Mary S), Propr Mulino Flour Mill, Agt Pac Tel & Tel Co, Postmaster (See Adv)
HOWARD CLAUD, Greenhouse (See Adv)
Howard Mary S Mrs, sec Oregon State Grange
HULT LUMBER CO, N P Hult Pres, J. Philip Hult Sec, Oscar N Hult Treas-Gen Mngr (See Adv)
Hult N P (Ida), pres Hult Lumber Co
Hult Oscar N (Olive), treas-gen mngr Hult Lumber Co
Hult Philip (Henrietta), sec Mulino Development Co and Hult Lumber Co
JEPSON J N, (Marian), Dry Goods, Groceries, Shoes, Drugs, Farm Produce (See Adv)
Jepson Annie, clerk J N Jepson
Jepson Marinus, clerk J N Jepson
Knightly & Mallet, real estate
Lutheran church
Maples Edon J, justice of the peace
Mulino Development Co, Philip Hult sec
MULINO FLOUR MILL, C T Howard Prop (See Adv)
Mulino Hotel, A Erickson propr
Mulino Public School, Flora Grice, teacher
Mulino Telephone Co, Vesta B Churchill opr
Mulino Water Co, B A Howard sec-treas
Nordling G J (Anna), bkpr Hult Lumber Co
OLSON AUGUST, Livery and Feed Stable (See Adv)
POSTOFFICE, C T Howard, Postmaster
McConahy E B, agt W V S Ry
SCOTT ALEXANDER (Elizabeth)
Scott I D, clerk
Snodgrass R H, live stock dealer

A 1916 Clackamas County Directory depicts the thriving town of Mulino including a "Mulino Hotel" operated by A. Erickson. This was probably a boarding house operated by August and Josie Erickson in a large, eight, bedroom house that stood where the PGE power plant is now just southeast of Milk Creek Bridge. The house was also used as an early stagecoach stop. The Ericksons also operated one of the early Mulino grocery stores.

Around 1905, the Howards donated land for a church building.

Early Town Platted

In 1912, the Mulino Townsite Company was formed by a Mr. J. W. Bowman and Associates, of Portland, and sixty acres of land were purchased from Charles Howard. This land was platted into town lots and a formal opening of the new town of Mulino was had. The opening day, which was attended by the populace for many miles around, was made a gala occasion with a big barbecue being one of the features.

The Townsite Company donated a block of ground for school purposes, and bonds were voted for the erection of a school building. A one room school was built where the present school is now, north of Passmore Road. This school was used until 1916 when a new two room school was built with full basement and indoor plumbing. The school district bought an acre from J. D. Daniels and moved the old one room school to the back of the school grounds and it was used as a playshed until one of the early teachers bought the building and it was moved. Rumor has it that this little building was added onto a house in Mulino and is still around today. The two room school building was replaced and in 1971, Sid Gasser, local visionary, had the old two-room building moved to his property in Mulino, with hopes of eventually restoring it.

In 1912, the business and manufacturing interests of Mulino consisted of two stores, the flour and feed mill, a saw mill, a shingle mill and a blacksmith shop. With the prospect of the Willamette Valley Southern arriving the next year, the growth of Mulino seemed impossible to thwart.

In 1914, Charles Howard had an interesting brochure printed advertising land in Mulino: "Lots for sale on easy terms. At Mulino, on the Willamette Valley Southern Railway, first class new electric line, 4 trains daily each way. Lots nearly all level, easy and cheap drainage, only $40 and up. C. T. Howard, Mulino, Oregon, owner." Obviously, C. T. was ahead of his time with innovations of advertising.

Charles Howard helped to bring good water into the homes of Mulino from the springs on the east hill. He was also involved in the Willamette Valley Southern Railway, which came through Mulino in 1913. Mulino had two railway stations: one at the foot of the Mulino hill on Highway 213 called Howard Station and another located on the county road to Canby near the community hall called Mulino Station. It was large and all the freight and mail came here. A railroad spur ran parallel to Milk Creek behind the homes on the east side of Highway 213 going to the Hult's Saw Mill and across the highway to the Howard's Grist Mill.

Charles and Mary's Children

To Charles and Mary were born two sons: Claude and Bayne. Claude operated a greenhouse and was agent at Mulino for the Willamette Valley Southern Railroad. He

In 1914, Charles T. Howard had an interesting brochure printed advertising land in Mulino: "Lots for sale on easy terms. At Mulino, on the Willamette Valley Southern Railway, first class new electric line, 4 trains daily each way. Lots nearly all level, easy and cheap drainage, only $40 and up. C. T. Howard, Mulino, Oregon, owner." These pictures show a new business block, Hult Lumber Company, Howard's Grist Mill on Milk Creek and the old Howard family home.

In front of the residence are C. T. and Mary Howard with their daughter-in-law Lillian Gans Howard standing by the fence and her two children Lorna and Burrell sitting on the lawn. The building at the top of the picture at one time contained a meat market, store, barber shop and bath. Presently it is the home of the Mulino Grange on South Mulino Road.

Mulino School classes were held in the first Mulino Grange Hall, built in 1876. Identified in this 1894 picture are; front row from the left the first (plaid dress) and third little girls are Florence and Kattie Daniels, Albert Erickson is the last boy on the right hand side of the front row and Jot Mallott is the fourth boy from the right in the front row with Charlie Daniels immediately to the right-back of him. The ladies on the right hand side of the picture - starting from the right are Mary Daniels, Josie Erickson and Kate Manning with Elmer Erickson standing in front of her. Bayne Howard is the tall boy in the middle of the back row and the lady on the horse in back is Mrs. John Darnell. Others are unidentified. *Photo courtesy of Blanche Daniels Engle.*

never married. When Charles passed away in 1923, Bayne took over operation of the grist mill.

Bayne was born in 1883 and for two and a half years attended school at Mulino. For one term he was a student at Woodburn and at an early age started to work in his father's grist mill, mastering every detail of the business. During 1905 he was employed on a Columbia River seining ground and the balance of his business career was spent in the mill. The production of flour was discontinued about 1924, although the mill still ground other grains and the plant became chiefly devoted to the manufacture of mixed feed, sold in large quantities to the poultry raisers and dairymen of the region. The mill remained in operation until 1944, when Union Mills took it over. Bayne Howard worked for Union Mills until his retirement.

In 1908, Bayne married Lillian Gans, daughter of Henry Gans. They had two children; Lorna A. and Burrell G.

Lillian Gans Howard passed away in 1915. Because of the Howard's support of the railroad system, Willamette Valley Southern, upon the death of Lillian, they allowed her body to be taken for cremation to Portland on the new train. In 1920, Bayne married Estella A. Riley, daughter of William and Mary Ellen Riley.

The Other Howard Children

Francis Turner Howard (b. 1830) married Ann Augusta Wingfield in 1851 and their children were: Elizabeth Cynthia (b. 1852, d. 1854), Eugenia Ellen (b. 1858, m. Charles Seefred), Juliet Francis (b. 1854, m. Daniel Newton Trullinger) and Edwin Albert (b. 1856, m. Mary Louise Morris of the Klinger family). Francis, known as Frank, was a farmer. Ann and Francis drowned together, in 1864, when their wagon overturned crossing a flood-swollen Molalla River about a mile south of the present bridge. Their minor children were reared by Robert and Lucy Wingfield Worsham in Canemah, Oregon.

William Howard was a minister and never married.

John Howard was a farmer, minister and school superintendent for Douglas County, Oregon, from 1882-1884. He married Ann's sister, Jane Elizabeth Wingfield. They had two children: Mary J. (b. 1855, m. J. Fletcher

The Francis Turner Howard family. Top photo is of Edwin Albert and Francis Turner Howard. Bottom photo is from left: Eugenia Ellen, Ann Augusta Wingfield Howard and Juliet Francis. ca. 1860. *Photos courtesy of Barbara Howard Hostetler.*

This 1920 s picture is of the two room school house built in 1916 that was moved in 1971 to Sid Gasser's place on Highway 213 in Mulino. Students are identified in the picture on the opposite page. *Photo courtesy of Barbara Howard Hostetler.*

Coates) and Martha E. (b. 1860).

Sarah Howard married Eli Casey Officer, son of James and Eveline Cooley Officer. Their children were Josephine (b. 1857, m. John A. Laycock), Louisa (b. 1859, m. Elmer Oliver Aldrich who was killed by Indians, then m. William Eddy) and Sarah Ann (b. 1861, m. Sam Miller, then Eminger "Billy" Stewart). The mother, Sarah, died from complications of childbirth and after her death, Eli Officer married three more times - Mary Jane Woods Thorpe in 1862, Mary Ann Blaylock in 1879, and Mary A. Round in 1892 - and had many children from these marriages.

Anna Howard (b. 1846) married Adam Weatherstone, a millwright, and had children William (b. 1863) and Lillie (b. 1867).

Anthony Wayne Howard (b. 1857) married and divorced Annie E. Ganong. They had one son, Thornton. Anthony was a clerk in a drygoods store and ran an excelsior mill.

Three children - Daniel Boone Howard (b. 1844, d. 1845), Mary M. Howard (b. 1849, d. 1854) and Grace Howard (b.1852, d. 1852) - died in childhood of acute dysentery or as it was called then "the bloody flux".

Mulino Today

As originally constructed, Howard's Grist Mill was a one and one-half story frame structure 33 by 44 feet. When electric turbines were installed at the mill in the early 1930s, the millrace was filled in and the water wheel

Mulino Grade School, 1920. Row 1, from left; Blanche Daniels, Alfred Holstein, Gertrude Allen, Esther Erickson, Dorothy Erickson, Marion Goldson, Helen Parks, Laura Kappler. Row 2, from left; Dick Waldorf, Blanche Erickson, Daisy Manning, Donald Daniels, Raymond Manning, Helen Brady. Row 3, from left; Elvin Erickson, Virgil Erickson, Ernest Harding, Burrell Howard, Lee Daniels, Paul Wallace, Albert Wallace and one unidentified child. Row 4, from left; Leonard Manning, Arthur Clauson, Gordon Perry, Laurence Brady, Ward Garrett, Lester Faulver, Juanita Hult, Bernice Erickson. Row 5, from left; Cora Cash, Violet Manning, Lorna Howard, Lillian Waldorf, Lidia Mallott. Row 6, from left; Ethel Bounds, Arleta Smith, unknown Cash, Mabel Bounds, Fred Clauson, Elvin Davis, John Lombard, Carl Clauson. Row 7, from left; Teacher Miss Grace Schuebel, Jesse Howard, unidentified, Grover Adkins, Weldon Erickson, Vance Murrey, Teacher Mr. Lundstrom. *Photo courtesy of Blanche Daniels Engle.*

---

removed. Some records say that the old millstones were buried at the bottom of the fill. Despite alterations to the mill over the years - 1890, 1900, 1930 and 1970 - the original framing members, flooring and square nails are still visible.

Today, Mulino remains an unincorporated town, with the school, Grange and Lions Club the hub of the community. Howard's Grist Mill is on the National Historic Register and in the summer of 1991, seven other Mulino structures were given Clackamas County Landmark status by the

Clackamas County Board of Commissioners. Those seven structures are the Milk Creek Bridge, the Mulino Baptist Church, the Charles T. and Mary Howard House, the Walter and Calla Waldorf House, the Howard-Waldorf Blacksmith Shop, the Charles T. & Mary Howard Farm and the George and Annie Force House.

Against improbable odds, Mulino remains a "step back in time".

*   *   *

The Mannings operated this Mulino Store about 1900. It was west of where the Mulino church now is on the old road. Passerbys may have noticed a narrow strip of pavement on this road. This type of pavement was used in the early days and if two vehicles met on the road one would have to move off the pavement to let the other pass. Frank Manning, Sr. is the man standing with the beard and Frank Manning, Jr. is in the wagon. The girls on the porch are from left: Edith, Mary and Calla Manning. Note the netting on the horses that was used to keep flys off. *Photo courtesy of Nita Kimmel.*

Author's Acknowledgements

The author gratefully acknowledges these descendants of early families who contributed family photographs of their ancestors:

The Vaughans of Molalla
Champ Clark Vaughan of Portland, Oregon

The Wrights of Liberal
Agnes Wright Crawford of Molalla, Oregon
Bertha Wright Nolan of Milwaukie, Oregon
George Wright of Hillsboro, Oregon

The Engles of Molalla
Blanche Daniels Engle of Mulino, Oregon
the late Ed Engle of Molalla, Oregon

The Klingers of Macksburg
the late Marie Klinger Bird of Macksburg, Oregon
Dorothy Felix of Colton, Oregon

The Trullingers of Union Mills
Alvin Friedrich of Canby, Oregon

The Bagbys of Wilhoit
Wilma Novak of Molalla, Oregon

The Dibbles & The Sawtells of Molalla
Neta Garley of Portland, Oregon

The Robbins & The Shavers of Molalla
Gena Cline of Molalla, Oregon

The Harless and Ogle Mountain Mine Story
Mildred Harless of Molalla, Oregon

The Howards of Mulino
Barbara Howard Hostetler of Portland, Oregon

With a special thank you to:

The late Mrs. Homer Stipp of Molalla, Oregon, for contribution of photographs.
Mr. Richard Holmes of Liberal, Oregon, for assistance and contribution of photographs.
Delores Peterkin of Molalla, Oregon, for assistance and contribution of photographs.
Pacific First Bank of Molalla, Oregon, for contribution of photographs.
Jim Yoder of Canby, Oregon, for sharing his story of Needy, Oregon.
Ellen Wilfley of Molalla, Oregon, for contributions of photographs.
my friends at the Molalla Historical Society, especially Isabel Williams and Gena Cline
for all the support, encouragement and contribution of photographs.

& the following friends and employees who have assisted the past two and one-half years
with production and distribution of my historical newspaper "Everything's Fine-O in Mulino!":
Sarah Ashton, Bill Gambell, Jr., and Bob Nadeau of Mulino, Oregon
Nancy Silver of Nancy's Typesetting of Canby, Oregon
Joy Butchko, Carleen James and Frank Schmuck of Portland, Oregon